Build Supercomputers with Raspberry Pi 3

A step-by-step guide that will enhance your skills in creating powerful systems to solve complex issues

Carlos R. Morrison

BIRMINGHAM - MUMBAI

Build Supercomputers with Raspberry Pi 3

First published: March 2017

Production reference: 1210317

Published by Packt Publishing Ltd.
Livery Place
35 Livery Street
Birmingham
B3 2PB, UK.
ISBN 978-1-78728-258-2

www.packtpub.com

Credits

Author

Carlos R. Morrison

Reviewer

Dr. Isaiah M. Blankson

Commissioning Editor

Vijin Boricha

Acquisition Editor

Namrata Patil

Content Development Editor

Mamata Walkar

Technical Editor

Varsha Shivhare

Copy Editor

Safis Editing

Project Coordinator

Kinjal Bari

Proofreader

Safis Editing

Indexer

Tejal Daruwale Soni

Graphics

Kirk D'Penha

Production Coordinator

Melwyn Dsa

About the Author

Carlos R. Morrison was born in Kingston, Jamaica, West Indies. He received a B.S. (Hons) degree in physics with a mathematics minor in 1986 from Hofstra University, Hempstead, NY, and an M.S. degree in physics in 1989 from Polytechnic University, Brooklyn, NY.

In 1989, he joined the NASA Glenn Research Center, Cleveland, OH, as a staff scientist in the solid-state physics branch and, in 1999, he transferred to the structures and dynamics branch. He has authored and coauthored several journal and technical articles associated with aerospace and electromagnetic devices. He holds several patents, including one on the Morrison Motor for which he won the 2004 R&D 100 Award, and software technologies used to control magnetic bearings. He is currently engaged in research associated with room temperature and superconducting reluctance motors, and Simulink Simulation of said motors.

Mr. Morrison is a member of the American Physical Society and the National Technical Association.

I would like to thank Dr. Isaiah Blankson for reading the manuscript, and for building and testing the Pi cluster.

About the Reviewer

Dr. Isaiah M. Blankson received his PhD in Aeronautics and Astronautics from the Massachusetts Institute of Technology, Cambridge, MA, USA. He is a specialist in hypersonic aerodynamics and propulsion. His current research involves the use of computational (CFD) and experimental methods for **Magneto Hydrodynamic (MHD)** energy bypass engine concepts for space-access vehicles, and non-equilibrium plasma for applications in hypersonic aerodynamics and propulsion. Previously, he was an aerospace scientist at the **General Electric Global Research Center (CRD)** in Niskayuna, NY. He has several US patents, including one on an MHD-controlled turbojet engine for space access, and another on an exoskeletal gas-turbine engine. He is the author of numerous technical publications, and an associate fellow of the **American Institute of Aeronautics and Astronautics (AIAA)**. Over the years, he has received many awards, including the distinguished presidential rank award for sustained superior accomplishment in 2012. As chief scientist at IMB and associates LLC, he develops and tests small-platform supercomputers for solving complex engineering problems.

Here are some of the other books he has worked on:

- Reviewer of selected chapters: Book to be published (2017) by Cambridge University Press, UK
- *Plasma Physics for Engineering*, by Dr. Joseph J. S. Shang and Dr. Sergey T. Surzhikov

www.PacktPub.com

For support files and downloads related to your book, please visit www.PacktPub.com.

Did you know that Packt offers eBook versions of every book published, with PDF and ePub files available? You can upgrade to the eBook version at www.PacktPub.com and as a print book customer, you are entitled to a discount on the eBook copy. Get in touch with us at service@packtpub.com for more details.

At www.PacktPub.com, you can also read a collection of free technical articles, sign up for a range of free newsletters and receive exclusive discounts and offers on Packt books and eBooks.

https://www.packtpub.com/mapt

Get the most in-demand software skills with Mapt. Mapt gives you full access to all Packt books and video courses, as well as industry-leading tools to help you plan your personal development and advance your career.

Why subscribe?

- Fully searchable across every book published by Packt
- Copy and paste, print, and bookmark content
- On demand and accessible via a web browser

Customer Feedback

Thanks for purchasing this Packt book. At Packt, quality is at the heart of our editorial process. To help us improve, please leave us an honest review on this book's Amazon page at https://www.amazon.com/dp/1787282589.

If you'd like to join our team of regular reviewers, you can e-mail us at customerreviews@packtpub.com. We award our regular reviewers with free eBooks and videos in exchange for their valuable feedback. Help us be relentless in improving our products!

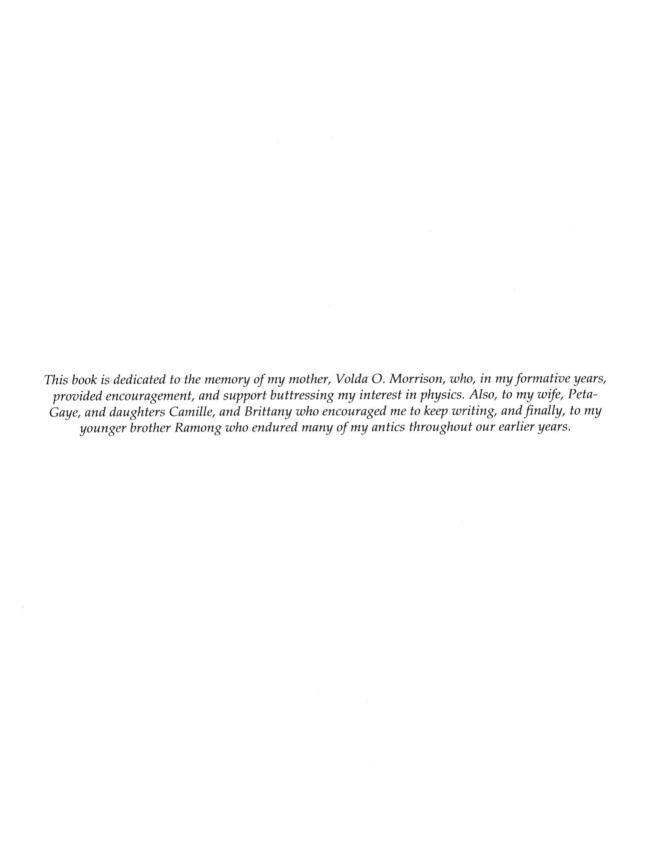

This book is dedicated to the memory of my mother, Volda O. Morrison, who, in my formative years, provided encouragement, and support buttressing my interest in physics. Also, to my wife, Peta-Gaye, and daughters Camille, and Brittany who encouraged me to keep writing, and finally, to my younger brother Ramong who endured many of my antics throughout our earlier years.

Table of Contents

Preface

This book explains how to build and operate a powerful eight or 16-node Pi2 or Pi3 supercomputer. You will be provided detailed systematic instructions on installing the Linux/Ubuntu operating system on your PC, and its use in configuring, communicating with, and ultimately operating your Pi supercomputer.

Initially, you will learn how to write and run a serial and a **Message Passing Interface (MPI)** π code on your PC, which is then used as a one-node supercomputer. Armed with this knowledge, you will then configure a Pi one-node, 4-core supercomputer on which you subsequently run the previous mentioned MPI π code. Next, you will assemble a two-node, 8-core Pi supercomputer on which, again, you will execute said MPI π code, and finally, you will construct an eight or 16-node Pi supercomputer, which you will employ to solve complex calculations incorporating the MPI construct.

What this book covers

Chapter 1, *Getting Started with Supercomputing*, provides an overall perspective on the concept of supercomputing. The chapter discusses Von Neumann's architecture, Flynn's classical taxonomy, a historical perspective on supercomputing, serial and parallel computing techniques, and justifications – including an analytical perspective – for greater processing speeds.

Chapter 2, *One Node Supercomputing*, discusses how to do supercomputing on one node, in this instance, your PC. You will be instructed how to install Linux/Ubuntu on your PC, which you will then use to run a serial and MPI π code. Next, you will learn about the critical for loop construct that is used to assign tasks among the cores/processes. Finally, you will write/copy, and run/generate π from the MPI Euler, Leibniz, and Nilakantha infinite series.

Chapter 3, *Preparing the Initial Two Nodes*, discusses how to build a two-node Pi supercomputer. Initially, you will be presented with a list of parts. You will then learn about the origin of the Pi microcomputer, and its technical specs. Next, you will be shown how to configure the master node in preparation for transferring the requisite MPI test codes from your PC to the master node. Finally, you will configure the first slave node in preparation for the creation a two-node (master and slave1) supercomputer.

Chapter 4, *Static IP Address and Hosts File Setup*, discusses how to configure the static IP address of the master, slave1, and network switch. Next, you will learn how to set up the hosts file.

Chapter 5, *Creating a Common User for All Nodes*, discusses how to create a new user for the master node, how to create a password for the new user on the master node, how to create a new user for the slave1 node, and how to create a password for the new user on the slave1 node. In addition, you will learn how to generate a special key on the master node, which is required for seamless transitioning between the nodes without using a password. You will then learn how to copy the special key from the master node to the slave1 node. Next, you will edit the .bashrc file on the master node to facilitate seamless special key access to all the nodes. Finally, you will learn how to use the which command.

Chapter 6, *Creating a Mountable Drive on the Master Node*, discusses how to use the mkdir command to make a directory/folder, the chown command for changing ownership of the export drive from the root user to a new user, and the rpcbind command, which allows the master Pi to export the export drive on the master to slave nodes. You will learn how to edit the exports file, which at facilitates exporting the export drive on the master node to the slave nodes, use the nfs-kernel-server command; edit the bootup script rc.local, which will make the export drive on the master node mountable for use by the slave nodes; use the mount command to manually mount the export drive containing the MPI codes; use the cat command to display the content of a file; use the cp -a command to copy files/codes to the export drive; and use the -H command to task any or all nodes; and cores to work on a given problem.

Chapter 7, *Configuring the Eight Nodes*, discusses how to configure the eight or 16-node Pi supercomputer. You will be shown how to edit the fstab file on the slave1 node to set up an automatic mount command, the rc.local file on the slave1 node to automatically mount the export drive containing the MPI test code folder, the hosts files on the master and slave1 nodes to reflect the temporary IP address, and host names on the remaining six or fourteen slave nodes. You will then be shown how to use the **SD formatter for Windows** to format the remaining slave SD cards, and **win32 Disk Imager** to copy the slave1 SD card image to the remaining slave nodes in the cluster. You will then edit/update, once again, the hosts file on the master and slaves to reflect their actual IP addresses, edit the interfaces file on the super cluster nodes, and finally, update the MAC and IP address on the network switch for the remaining slave nodes.

Chapter 8, *Testing the Super Cluster*, discusses how to use the shutdown -h now command to shut down your Pi computer, the -H command to solve the MPI π function in record time, and create convenience bash files to enhance the user experience while operating the supercomputer.

Chapter 9, *Real-World Math Application*, discusses how to write and run serial and MPI Taylor series, sine, cosine, tangent, and the natural log functions.

Chapter 10, *Real-World Physics Application*, discusses how to write and run the MPI code for a vibrating string.

Chapter 11, *Real-World Engineering Application*, discusses how to write and run a serial and MPI sawtooth Fourier series code.

What you need for this book

You will need Linux/Ubuntu OS installed on your PC with the option to access the Windows OS, and a basic working knowledge of the C language.

Who this book is for

This book targets hobbyists and enthusiasts who want to explore building supercomputers with microcomputers. Researchers will also find this book useful. Prior programming knowledge is necessary; knowledge of supercomputers is not.

Conventions

In this book, you will find a number of text styles that distinguish between different kinds of information. Here are some examples of these styles and an explanation of their meaning. Code words in text, database table names, folder names, filenames, file extensions, pathnames, dummy URLs, user input, and Twitter handles are shown as follows: "How to use the shutdown -h now command to shut"

Any command-line input or output is written as follows:

```
alpha@Mst0:/beta/gamma $ time mpiexec -H
Mst0,Mst0,Mst0,Mst0,Slv1,Slv1,Slv1,Slv1,Slv2,Slv2 MPI_08_b
```

New terms and important words are shown in bold. Words that you see on the screen, for example, in menus or dialog boxes, appear in the text like this: "On a Windows 7 machine, click on **Systems & Security**, then click on **System**, then **Device Manage**r, and click on **Processor**."

Warnings or important notes appear in a box like this.

Tips and tricks appear like this.

Reader feedback

Feedback from our readers is always welcome. Let us know what you think about this book—what you liked or disliked. Reader feedback is important for us as it helps us develop titles that you will really get the most out of. To send us general feedback, simply e-mail feedback@packtpub.com, and mention the book's title in the subject of your message. If there is a topic that you have expertise in and you are interested in either writing or contributing to a book, see our author guide at www.packtpub.com/authors.

Customer support

Now that you are the proud owner of a Packt book, we have a number of things to help you to get the most from your purchase.

Downloading the example code

You can download the example code files for this book from your account at http://www.packtpub.com. If you purchased this book elsewhere, you can visit http://www.packtpub.com/support and register to have the files e-mailed directly to you.

You can download the code files by following these steps:

1. Log in or register to our website using your e-mail address and password.
2. Hover the mouse pointer on the **SUPPORT** tab at the top.
3. Click on **Code Downloads & Errata**.
4. Enter the name of the book in the **Search** box.
5. Select the book for which you're looking to download the code files.
6. Choose from the drop-down menu where you purchased this book from.
7. Click on **Code Download**.

Once the file is downloaded, please make sure that you unzip or extract the folder using the latest version of:

- WinRAR / 7-Zip for Windows
- Zipeg / iZip / UnRarX for Mac
- 7-Zip / PeaZip for Linux

The code bundle for the book is also hosted on GitHub at `https://github.com/PacktPubl ishing/Build-Supercomputers-with-Raspberry-Pi-3`. We also have other code bundles from our rich catalog of books and videos available at `https://github.com/PacktPublish ing/`. Check them out!

Downloading the color images of this book

We also provide you with a PDF file that has color images of the screenshots/diagrams used in this book. The color images will help you better understand the changes in the output. You can download this file from
`http://www.packtpub.com/sites/default/files/downloads/BuildSupercomputerswithRa spberryPi3_ColorImages.pdf`.

Errata

Although we have taken every care to ensure the accuracy of our content, mistakes do happen. If you find a mistake in one of our books—may be a mistake in the text or the code—we would be grateful if you could report this to us. By doing so, you can save other readers from frustration and help us improve subsequent versions of this book. If you find any errata, please report them by visiting http://www.packtpub.com/submit-errata, selecting your book, clicking on the **Errata Submission Form** link, and entering the details of your errata. Once your errata are verified, your submission will be accepted and the errata will be uploaded to our website or added to any list of existing errata under the **Errata** section of that title.

To view the previously submitted errata, go to https://www.packtpub.com/books/content/support and enter the name of the book in the search field. The required information will appear under the Errata section.

Piracy

Piracy of copyrighted material on the Internet is an ongoing problem across all media. At Packt, we take the protection of our copyright and licenses very seriously. If you come across any illegal copies of our works in any form on the Internet, please provide us with the location address or website name immediately so that we can pursue a remedy. Please contact us at copyright@packtpub.com with a link to the suspected pirated material. We appreciate your help in protecting our author and our ability to bring you valuable content.

Questions

If you have a problem with any aspect of this book, you can contact us at questions@packtpub.com, and we will do our best to address the problem.

1
Getting Started with Supercomputing

The prefix **super** in the moniker **supercomputer** may, to the ill-informed, conjure up images of the electronic supervillain HAL 9000 in Arthur C. Clarke's classic movie 2001: A Space Odyssey or the benevolent superhero Clark Kent, aka Superman, who inhabits the DC comic universe. However, the tag supercomputer is, in fact, associated with a non-fictional entity that has no ill-will towards humans – at least not at this moment in time. Supercomputing and supercomputers are the subject matter of this book.

In this chapter, we introduce the reader to the basics of supercomputing, or more precisely, parallel processing. Parallel processing is a computational technique that is currently enjoying widespread usage at many research institutions, including universities and government laboratories, where machines routinely carry out computation in the teraflops (1 billion floating point operations per second) and petaflops (1,000 teraflops) domain. Parallel processing significantly reduces the time needed to analyze and/or solve complex and difficult mathematical and scientific problems, such as weather prediction, where a daunting myriad of physical atmospheric conditions must be considered and processed simultaneously in order to obtain generally accurate weather forecasting.

Supercomputing is also employed in analyzing the extreme physical conditions extant at the origin of the much-discussed Big Bang event, in studying the dynamics of galaxy formation, and in simulating and analyzing the complex physics of atomic and thermonuclear explosions – data that is crucial to the military for maintaining and designing even more powerful weapons of mass destruction – holy crap!! This doesn't bode well for humanity. Anyway, these are just a few examples of tasks germane to parallel processing. Following are images of events that are being studied/simulated by scientist employing supercomputers:

| Galaxy Formation | Planetary Movments | Climate Change |

The enhanced processing speed, so central to parallel computing, is achieved by assigning chunks of data to different processors in a computer network, where the processors then concurrently execute similar, specifically designed code logic on their share of the data. The partial solution from each processor is then gathered to produce a final result. You will indeed be exploring this technique later when you run example codes on your PC, and then on your Pi2 or Pi3 supercomputer.

The computational time compression associated with parallel computing is typically on the order of a few minutes or hours, rather than weeks, months, or years. The sharing of tasks among processors is facilitated by a communication protocol for programming parallel computers called **Message Passing Interface (MPI)**. The MPI standard, which came to fruition between the 1980s and early 1990s, was finally ratified in 2012 by the MPI Forum, which has over 40 participating organizations.

You can visit `https://computing.llnl.gov/tutorials/mpi/` for a brief history and tutorial on MPI, and `https://computing.llnl.gov/tutorials/parallel_comp/` for parallel computing. You can also visit `http://mpitutorial.com/tutorials/` for additional information and a tutorial on MPI programming.

In this chapter, you will learn about the following topics:

- John von Neumann's stored-program computer architecture
- Flynn's classical taxonomy
- Historical perspective on supercomputing and supercomputers
- Serial processing techniques
- Parallel processing techniques
- The need for greater processing speed
- Additional analytical perspective on the need for greater processing speed

Von Neumann architecture

Dr. John von Neumann:

John von Neumann circa the 1940s

Any discussion concerning computers must include the contributions of the famed Hungarian mathematician/genius Dr. John von Neumann. He was the first to stipulate, in his famous 1945 paper, the general requirements for an electronic computer. This device was called a **stored-program computer**, since the data and program instructions are kept in electronic memory. The specification was a departure from earlier designs where computers were programmed via hard wiring. Von Neumann's basic design has endured to this day, as practically all modern-day processors exhibit some vestiges of this design architecture (see the following figure):

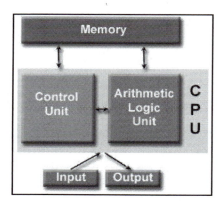

Von Neumann architecture

Von Neumann's design basic components are tabulated as follows:

- The four main elements:
    - A memory component
    - A controller unit
    - A logic unit for doing arithmetic
    - An input and output port

- A means for storing data and program instructions termed read/write random access memory
    - The data is information utilized by the program
    - The program instructions consist of coded data that guides the computer to complete a task
- **Controller Unit** acquires information from memory, deciphers the information, and then sequentially synchronizes processes to achieve the programmed task
- Basic arithmetic operations occur in the **Arithmetic Logic Unit**

- **Input** and **Output** ports allow access to the **Central Processing Unit (CPU)** by a human operator
- Additional information can be obtained at
  `https://en.wikipedia.org/wiki/John_von_Neumann`

So, how does this architecture relates to parallel processors/supercomputers? You might ask. Well, supercomputers consist of nodes, which are, in fact, individual computers. These computers contain processors with the same architectural elements described previously.

Flynn's classical taxonomy

Parallel computers can be classified in at least four ways:

- **Single Instruction stream Single Data stream (SISD)**
- **Single Instruction stream Multiple Data stream (SIMD)**
- **Multiple Instruction stream Single Data stream (MISD)**
- **Multiple Instruction stream Multiple Data stream (MIMD)**

These classifications are discussed in more detail in the `Appendix`:

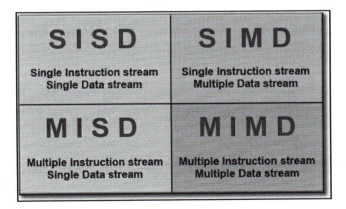

Michael J. Flynn proposed this classification in 1966, and it is still in use today. The Cray-1 and the CDC 7600 supercomputer discussed in the following sections are of the **SISD** class. Use the following link to learn more about Flynn:
`https://en.wikipedia.org/wiki/Flynn's_taxonomy.`

Historical perspective

The descriptor **super computing** first appeared in the publication New York World in 1929. The term was in reference to the large, custom-built IBM tabulator installed at Columbia University. The IBM tabulator is depicted following:

IBM Tabulators and Accounting Machine

The burgeoning supercomputing field was later buttressed with contributions from the famed Seymour Cray, with his brainchild, the CDC6600, that appeared in 1964. The machine, for all intents and purposes, was the first supercomputer. Cray was an applied mathematician, computer scientist, and electrical engineer. He subsequently built many faster machines. He passed away on October 5, 1996 (age 71) but his legacy lives on today in several powerful supercomputers bearing his name.

The quest for the exaflop machine (a billion, billion calculations per second) commenced when computer engineers in the 1980s gave birth to a slew of supercomputers that only had a few processors. In the 1990s, machines that had thousands of processors began appearing in the United States and Japan. These machines achieved new teraflop (1,000 billion calculations per second) processing performance records, but this achievement was only fleeting, as the end of the 20th century ushered in petaflop (1,000,000 billion calculations per second) machines that had large-scale parallel architecture. These machines comprise thousands (over 60,000, to give an estimate) of off-the-shelf processors similar to those used in personal computers. Indeed, progress in performance is relentless, and inexorable – maybe? I guess only time will tell. An image of an early trailblazing supercomputer, the Cray-1, is depicted in the following figure:

A Cray-1 supercomputer preserved at the Deutsches Museum

The relentless drive for ever-greater computing power began in earnest in 1957 when a splinter group of engineers left the Sperry Corporation to launched the Minneapolis, MN based **Control Data Corporation (CDC)**. In the subsequent year, the venerable Seymour Cray also left Sperry. He teamed up with the Sperry splinter group at CDC, and in 1960 the 48-bit CDC1604 – the first solid state computer – was presented to the world. It operated at 100,000 operations per second. It was a computational beast at the time, and certainly a unicorn in a world dominated by vacuum tubes.

Cray's CDC1604 was designed to be the apex machine of that era. However, after an additional 4 years of experimentation with colleagues Jim Thornton, Dean Roush, and 30 other Cray engineers, the 60-bit CDC6600 was born. The machine debuted in 1964. The development of the CDC 6600 was made possible when the company Fairchild Semiconductor delivered to Cray and his team the much faster compact germanium transistors, which were used in lieu of the slower silicon-based transistors. These faster, compact, germanium transistors, however, had a drawback, namely excessive heat generation. This problem was mitigated with refrigeration, an innovation pioneered by Dean Roush. Because the machine outperformed its contemporaries by a factor of 10, it was dubbed a supercomputer, and after selling 100 computers, each costing a stratospheric $8 million, the moniker has now become permanently etched in our collective consciousness for decades hence.

The 6600 achieved speed acceleration by outsourcing mundane work to associated computing peripherals, thus freeing up the CPU for actual data processing. The machine used the Minnesota FORTRAN compiler designed by Liddiard and Mundstock (both men were affiliated with the University of Minnesota). The compiler allowed the processor to operate at a sustained 500 kiloflops, or 0.5 megaflops, on sustained mathematical operations. The subsequent CDC7600 machine regained the mantle as the world's apex machine in 1968; it ran at 36.4 MHz (approximately 3.5 times faster than the 6600). The speed gain was achieved by using other technical innovations. Only 50 of the 7,600 machines were sold. The 7600 is depicted following:

CDC7600 serial number 1 (this figure shows two sides of the C-shaped chassis)

In 1972, Cray separated from CDC to embark on a new venture. However, two years after his departure from the company, CDC introduced the STAR-100, a computational behemoth at the time, capable of executing 100 megaflops of processing power. The Texas Instruments ASC machine was also a member of this computer family. These machines ushered in what's now known as vector processing, an idea inspired by the APL programming language of the 1960s.

In 1956, researchers at Manchester University in Great Britain began experimenting with MUSE, which was derived from microsecond engine. The goal was to design a computer that could achieve processing speeds in the realm of microsecond per instruction, approximately 1 million instructions per second. At the tail end of 1958, the British electrical engineering company Ferranti collaborated with Manchester University on the MUSE project that ultimately resulted in a computer named Atlas; see the following figure:

The University of Manchester Atlas in January 1963

Atlas was commissioned on December 7, 1962, approximately three years before the CDC 6600 made its appearance as the world's first supercomputer. At that time, the Atlas was the most powerful computer in England and, some might argue, the world, having a processing capacity of four IBM 7094s, about 2 MHz. Indeed, a common refrain then was that half of Britain's computing capacity would have been lost had Atlas gone offline at any time.

Additionally, Atlas ushered in the use of virtual memory and paging – technologies used to extend its memory. The Atlas technology also gave birth to the Atlas Supervisor, which was the Windows or MAC OS of the day.

The mid-1970s and 1980s are considered the Cray era. In 1976, Cray introduced the 80 MHz Cray-1. The machine affirmatively established itself as the most successful supercomputer in history. Cray engineers incorporated integrated circuits (with two gates per chip) into the computer architecture. The chips were also capable of vector processing, which introduced innovations such as chaining, a process whereby scalar and vector registers produce a short-term result, which is then immediately used, thus obviating additional memory references, which tends to lower processing speeds. In 1982, the 105 MHz Cray X-MP was introduced. The machine boasts a shared-memory parallel vector processor with enhanced chaining support, and multiple memory pipelines. The X-MP's three floating point pipelines execute simultaneously. In 1985, the Cray-2 (see the following figure) was introduced. It had four liquid cooled processors that were fully submerged in Fluorinert, which boiled during normal operation, as heat was removed from the processors via evaporative cooling:

A liquid-cooled Cray-2 Supercomputer

The Cray-2 processors ran at 1.9 gigaflops, but played a subordinate role to the record holder, the Soviet Union's M-13, which operated at 2.4 gigaflops; see the following figure:

M13 Supercomputer, 1984

The M13 was dethroned in 1990 by the 10-gigaflop ETA-10G, courtesy of CDC. See the following figure:

CDC, ETA-10G Supercomputer

The 1990s saw the growth of massively parallel computing. Leading the charge was the Fujitsu Numerical Wind Tunnel supercomputer. The machine had 166 vector processors that propelled it to the apex of computational prowess in 1994. Each of the 166 processors operated at 1.7 gigaflops. However, the Hitachi SR2201, which had a distributed memory parallel system, bested the Fujitsu machine by chiming in at 614 gigaflops in 1996. The SR2201 used 2,048 processors that were linked together by a fast three-dimensional crossbar network.

The Intel Paragon, which was a contemporary of the SR2201, had 4,000 Intel i860 processors in varied configuration, and was considered the premier machine, with lineage dating back to 1993. Additionally, the Paragon used **Multiple Instructions Multiple Data (MIMD)** architecture, which linked processors together by way of a fast two-dimensional mesh. This configuration allows processes to run on multiple nodes (see the `Appendix`), using MPI. The Intel Paragon XP-E is shown here:

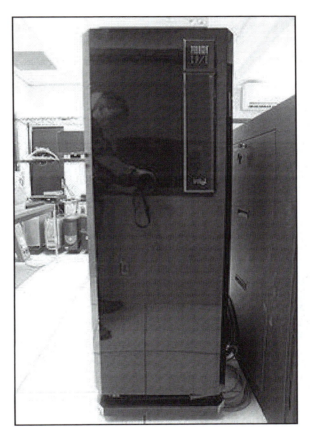

Intel Paragon XP-E single cabinet system Cats

The progeny of the Paragon architecture was the intel ASCI Red supercomputer (see the following figure). **Advanced Simulation and Computing Initiative (ASIC)**. The Red was installed at the Sandia National Laboratories in 1996, to help maintain the United States' nuclear arsenal pursuant to the 1992 memorandum on nuclear testing. The computer occupied the top spot of supercomputing machines through the end of the 20th century. The computer was massively parallel, bristling with over 9,000 computing nodes, and had more than 12 terabytes of data storage. The machine incorporated off-the-shelf Pentium Pro processors that had widely inhabited personal computers of the era. This computer punched through the 1 teraflop benchmark, ultimately reaching the new 2 teraflops benchmark:

ASCI Red supercomputer

Human desire for greater computing power entered the 21st century unabated. Petascale computing has now become the norm. A petaflop is 1 quadrillion floating point operations per second, which is 1,000 teraflops, which is 1,000,000,000,000,000 floating point operations per second, or 1×10^{15} flops. What?! Is there an end somewhere to this madness? It should be noted that greater computing capacity usually means greater consumption of energy, which translates to greater stress on the environment. The Cray C90, which debuted in 1991, consumed 500 kilowatts of power. The ASCI Q gobbled down 3,000 kW and was 2,000 times faster than the C90 a 300-fold performance per watt increase. Oh well!

In 2004, NEC's Earth Simulator supercomputer (see the following figure) achieved 35.9 teraflops, or $35.9 \times 1,000,000,000,000$ flops, that is, 39.5×10^{12} flops, using 640 nodes:

NEC Earth Simulator

IBM's contribution to the teraflop genre was the Blue Gene supercomputer (see the following figure):

Blue Gene/P supercomputer at Argonne National Laboratory

The Blue Gene supercomputer debuted in 2007, and operated at 478.2 teraflops. Its architecture was widely used in the former part of the 21st century. Blue Gene is, essentially, an IBM project whose mission was to design supercomputers with an operating speed in the realm of petaflops, but consuming relatively low power. At first glance, this might seem an oxymoron, but IBM achieved this by employing large numbers of low-speed processors that can then be air-cooled. This computational beast uses more than 60,000 processors, which are stacked 2,048 processors per rack. The racks are interconnected in a three-dimensional torus lattice. The IBM Roadrunner maxed out at 1.105 petaflops.

China has seen rapid progress in supercomputing technology. In June 2003, China placed 51st on the TOP500 list. This list is a worldwide ranking of the world's 500 fastest supercomputers. In November 2003, China moved up the ranks to 14th place. In June 2004, it moved to fifth place, ultimately attaining first place in 2010 with the Tianhe-1 supercomputer. The machine operated at 2.56 petaflops. Then, in July 2011, the Japanese K computer achieved 10.51 petaflops, thereby attaining the top spot. The machine employed over 60,000 SPARC64 V111fx processors encased in over 600 cabinets. In 2012, the IBM Sequoia came online, operating at 16.32 petaflops. The machine's residence is the Lawrence Livermore National Laboratory, California, USA. In the same year, the Cray Titan clocked in at 17.59 petaflops. This machine resides at the Oak Ridge National Laboratory, Tennessee, USA. Then, in 2013, the Chinese unveiled the NUDT Tianhe-2 supercomputer, which had a clock speed of 33.86 petaflops, and in 2016, the Sunway TaihuLight supercomputer came online in Wuxi, China. This machine now sits atop the heap with a processing speed of 93 petaflops. This latest achievement, however, must be considered fleeting, as historical trends dictate that more powerful machines are waiting in the wings to emerge soon. Case in point, on July 29, 2015, President Obama issued an executive order to build a super machine that will clock in at a whopping 1,000 petaflops, or one exaflop, approximately 30 times faster than Tianhe-2, and approximately 10 times faster than the newly minted Sunway TaihuLight supercomputer. Stay tuned, the race continues. The following figures show the five fastest machines on the planet to date. These images are presented in ascending order of processing speed, starting with the K computer. The following figure depicts the fifth fastest supercomputer, the K computer:

K computer

The following figure depicts the fourth fastest supercomputer, the IBM Sequoia:

IBM Sequoia

The following figure depicts the third fastest supercomputer, the Cray Titan:

Cray Titan

The following figure depicts the second fastest supercomputer, the Tianhe-2:

NUDT Tianhe-2

The following figure depicts the fastest supercomputer, the Sunway TaihuLight:

Sunway TaihuLight

Now, you might be asking yourself, so what is the process behind parallel computing? We briefly touched on this topic earlier, but now we will dig a little deeper. Let's examine the following figures, which should help you understand the mechanics behind parallel processing. We begin with the mechanics of serial processing.

Serial computing technique

The following figure shows a typical/traditional serial processing sequence:

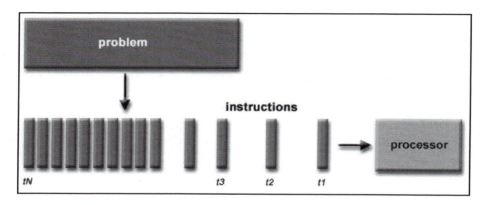

General serial processing

Serial computing traditionally involves the following:

- Breaking up the problem into chunks of instructions
- Sequentially executing the instructions
- Using a single processor to execute the instructions
- Executing the instructions one at a time

The following figure shows an actual application of serial computing. In this case, the payroll is being processed:

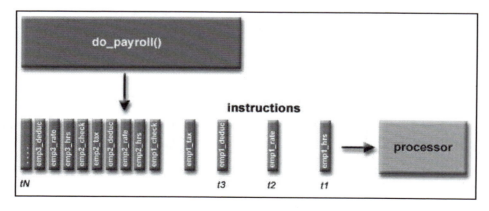

Example of payroll serial processing

Parallel computing technique

The following figure shows a typical sequence in parallel processing, where there is simultaneous use of multiple compute resources employed to solve a given problem:

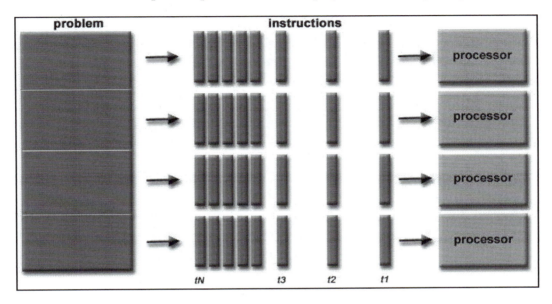

General parallel processing

Parallel computing involves the following:

- Breaking up the problem into portions that can be concurrently solved
- Breaking down each portion into a sequence of instruction sets
- Simultaneously executing each portion's instruction sets on multiple processors
- Using an overarching control/coordination scheme

- The following figure shows an actual application of parallel computing wherein the payroll is being processed:

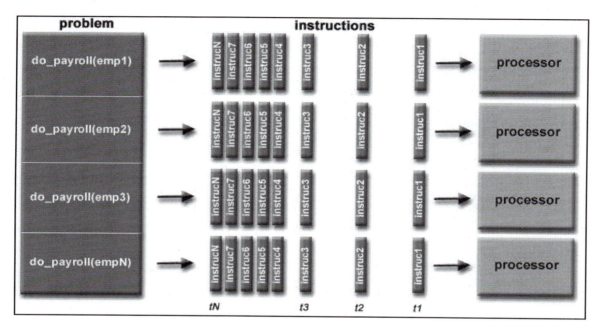

Example payroll parallel processing

One thing to note is that a given computational problem must be able to do the following:

- Be broken into smaller discrete chunks to be solved simultaneously
- Execute several program instructions at any given moment
- Be solved in a smaller time period, employing many compute resources, as compared to using a lone compute resource

Compute resources usually consist of the following:

- A sole computer possesses several processors or cores
- Any number of computers/processors linked together via a network

Modern computers contain processors with multiple cores (see `Appendix`), typically four cores (some processors have up to 18 cores, such as the IBM BG/Q Compute Chip), making it possible to run a parallel program using MPI on a single computer/PC or node – if it is part of a supercomputer cluster (see `Appendix`). This one-node supercomputing capability will be explored later in the book when you are instructed on running a simple parallelized π code. These processor cores also have several functional units, such as L1 cache, L2 cache, prefetch, branch, floating-point, decode, integer, graphics processing (GPU), and so on. The following figure shows a typical supercomputing cluster (see `Appendix`) network:

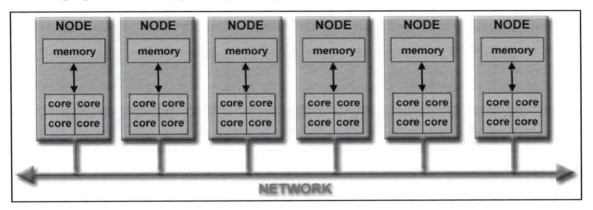

Example of a typical supercomputing network

These clusters can comprise several thousand nodes. The Blue Gene supercomputer discussed earlier has over 60,000 processors. The diminutive Raspberry Pi supercomputer has eight nodes comprising 32 cores (4 cores per Pi), or 16 nodes comprising 64 cores of processing capability. Since each node provides 4 GHz (4.8 GHz for Pi3) of processing power, your machine possesses 32 GHz (32×10^9) or (76.8 GHz for Pi3) of processing capacity. One can argue that this little machine is indeed superior to some supercomputers of yesteryear. At this point, it should be obvious why the technique of parallel processing is superior, in most instances, to serial computing.

The need for greater processing speed

The world/universe is an immensely parallel entity, wherein numerous complex, interconnected events are occurring simultaneously, and within a temporal sequence. Serially analyzing the physics/mechanics of these events would indeed take a very long time. On the other hand, parallel processing is highly suited for modeling and/or simulating these types of phenomena, such as the physics of nuclear weapons testing and galaxy formation mentioned earlier. Depicted here are additional events that lend themselves to parallel processing:

| Auto Assembly | Jet Construction | Drive-thru Lunch |
| Rush Hour Traffic | Plate Tectonics | Weather |

We have already discussed, in general, some of the reasons for employing parallel computing. Now we will discuss the main reasons. Let's start with saving money and time. It is, by and large, a truism that applying more resources to a task tends to accelerate its completion. The technique of parallel processing does indeed buttress this notion by applying multiple nodes/cores to the problem at hand – many hands make light work, to reprise an old adage. Additionally, parallel machines can be constructed from relatively cheap components.

Next up is the issue of needing to solve large, difficult, and complicated problems. Some problems are so enormously complicated and seemingly intractable that it would be foolhardy to attempt a solution with the processing power of a single computer, considering the computer's limited memory capacity. Some of the grand challenges for supercomputing can be found at this link: `https://en.wikipedia.org/wiki/Grand_Challenges`. These challenges require petaflops and petabytes of storage capacity. Search engines such as Google, Yahoo, and so on employ supercomputers to aid with processing millions of Internet searches and transactions occurring every second.

Concurrency produces greater processing speed. A lone computer processes one task at a time. However, by networking several lone computers, several tasks can be performed simultaneously. An example of this ethos is Collaborative Network, which offers a global virtual space for people to meet and work.

Next, non-local resources can play an important role in parallel processing. For example, when compute resources are inadequate, one can leverage the capacity of a wide area network, or the Internet. Another example of distributive computing is `SETI@home`, `http://setiathome.berkeley.edu/`. The network has millions of users worldwide, who provide their computer resources to help in the **Search for Extraterrestrial Intelligence (SETI)**. Incidentally, the author has been a member of SETI for several years running. Whenever he is not using his PC, it automatically lends its processing power to the organization. Another parallel computing organization is `Folding@home`, `http://folding.stanford.edu/`. Members provide their PC processor resource to help with finding a cure for Alzheimer's, Huntington's, Parkinson's, and many cancers.

Another, and final, reason for needing parallel computing is to effectively leverage the underlying parallel hardware for improved performance. The current crop of PCs, including laptops, house processors that have multiple cores that are configured in a parallel fashion. Parallel software, such as OpenMPI, is uniquely designed for processors with multiple cores, threads, and so on. You will be using OpenMPI later during the testing and running of your Raspberry Pi supercomputer. Running serial programs on your PC is essentially a waste of its computing capability. The following figure depicts a modern processor architecture by Intel:

Intel Xenon processor with six cores and six L3 cache units

What does the future hold? You might ask. Well, historical trends dictate that even more powerful supercomputers will emerge in the future – a trend that is guaranteed to continue – as chip-making technology unceasingly improves. In addition, faster network switches are evolving somewhat concurrently with the chips/processors. Switches are used for interconnecting the nodes in the supercomputer. The theoretical upper limit of processing speed on a supercomputer is impacted not only by the communication speed between the cores in the chip, but also by the communication speed between the nodes, and the network switch connecting the nodes. Faster network switching translates to faster processing. Parallelism as a concept is here to stay, and the associated technology is getting better and stronger as we go forward. The following figure depicts the supercomputing performance trend. The race for exaflop computing continues unabated:

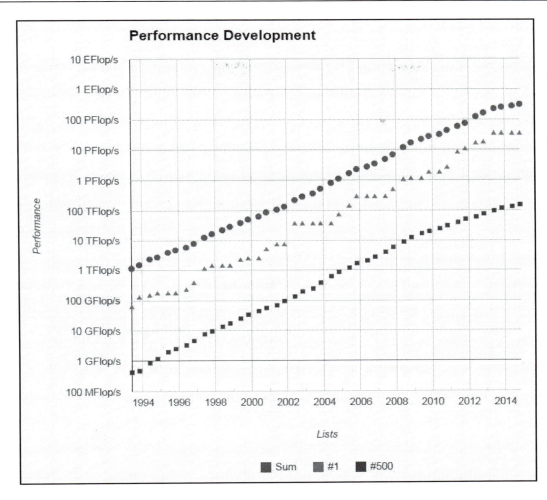

Supercomputing performance trend

The question you might be asking now is, who is using this awesome technology? Well, the short answer is tons of organizations and people. The group that are firmly on this list are scientist and engineers. Among the problem areas being studied/modeled by these eggheads are the following:

- Environment, earth, and atmosphere
- Applied physics: nuclear, particle, condensed matter, high pressure, fusion, and photonics
- Genetics, bioscience, and biotechnology
- Molecular science and geology

- Mechanical engineering
- Microelectronics, circuit design, and electrical engineering
- Mathematics and computer science
- Weapons and defense

The preceding list represents a few additional example applications of parallel computing. The following figure depicts additional applications of parallel processing in science and engineering:

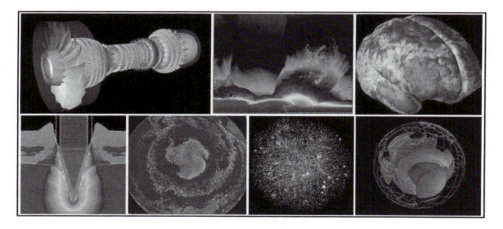

Images of engineering and scientific problems being modeled by supercomputers

The industrial sector is also a big user of supercomputing technology. Companies process huge amounts of data to improve product yield and efficiency. Some examples of this activity are as follows:

- Data mining, databases, big data
- Oil exploration
- Web-based business services and web search engines
- Medical diagnosis and medical imaging
- Pharmaceutical design
- Economic and financial modeling
- Management of national and multinational corporations
- Advanced graphics and virtual reality
- Multimedia technologies and networked video
- Collaborative work environments

The following figure depicts a few additional examples of industrial and commercial applications:

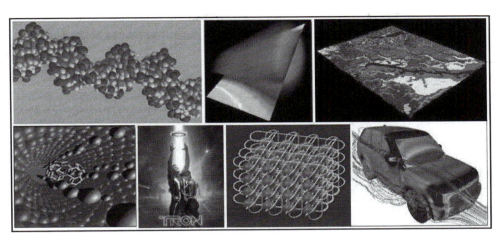

Images of commercial application of supercomputers

Globally, parallel computing is used in a wide variety of sectors; see the following graph:

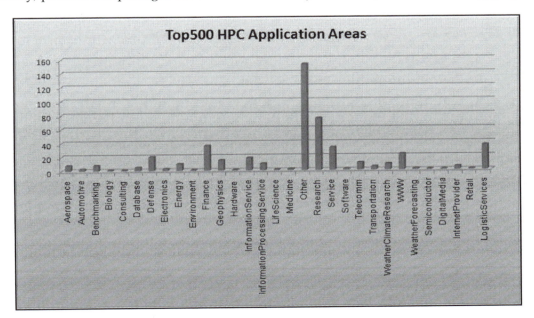

Worldwide use of supercomputing resources

Additional analytical perspective

Another perspective on why we need more computing power, goes as follows: let us supposed we want to predict the weather over an area covering the United States, and Canada. We cover the region with a cubical grid that extends 20 km over sea level, and examine the weather at each vertex of the grid. Now, suppose we use a cubic component of the grid that is 0.1 kilometer on the sides, and since the area of the United States, and Canada is approximately 20 million square kilometers. We therefore would need at least

$2.0 \times 10^7 km^2 \times 20\ km \times 10^3\ cubes\ per\ km^3 = 4 \times 10^{11} grid\ points$ let us also assume we need a minimum of 100 calculations to ascertain the weather condition at a grid point, then the weather, one hour hence, will require $4 \times 10^{11} \times 10^2 = 4 \times 10^{13}$ calculations. Now, to predict the weather hourly for the next 48 hours, we will need

$4 \times 10^{13}\ calculations \times 48\ hours \approx 2 \times 10^{15}\ calculations$. Assuming our serial computer can process 10^9 (one billion) calculations per second, it will take approximately

$(2 \times 10^{15}\ calculations) / (10^9\ calculations per\ second) = 2 \times 10^6\ seconds \approx 23\ days$! . Clearly, this is not going to work to our benefit if the computer is going to predict the weather at a grid point in 23 days. Now, suppose we can flip a switch that turbocharges our computer to perform 10^{12} (1 trillion) calculations per second; it would now take approximately half an hour to determine the weather at a grid point, and the weather guy can now make a complete prediction in the next 48 hours.

Outside of weather prediction, there are numerous other conditions/events occurring in the real world/universe that require a higher rate of calculation. This would require our computer to have a much higher processing speed in order to solve a given problem in a reasonable time. It is this nettling fact that is driving engineers and scientist to pursue higher and higher computational power. This is where parallel computing/supercomputing, with its associated MPI codes, excels. However, obstacles to widespread adaption of parallelism abound, courtesy of the usual suspects: hardware, algorithms, and software.

With regards to hardware, the network intercommunication pathway, aka switches, are falling behind the technology of the modern processor, in terms of communication speed. Slow switches negatively impact the theoretical upper computational speed limit of a supercomputer. You will observe this phenomenon when running your Pi supercomputer, as you bring successive nodes online that transition the input ports on the HP switch. Switch technology is improving, though not fast enough.

Processing speed is dependent on how fast a parallel code executes on the hardware, hence software engineers are designing faster and more efficient parallel algorithms that will boost the speed of supercomputing. Faster algorithms will boost the popularity of parallelism.

Finally, the most impactful obstacle to widespread adoption of parallelism is inadequate software. To date, compilers that can automatically parallelize sequential algorithms are limited in their applicability, and programmers are resigned to providing their own parallel algorithm.

Sources for reference

- https://computing.llnl.gov/tutorials/mpi/
- https://computing.llnl.gov/tutorials/parallel_comp/
- https://en.wikipedia.org/wiki/History_of_supercomputing
- http://www.columbia.edu/cu/computinghistory/tabulator.html
- https://en.wikipedia.org/wiki/CDC_1604
- http://www.icfcst.kiev.ua/MUSEUM/Kartsev.html
- http://www.icfcst.kiev.ua/MUSEUM/PHOTOS/M13.html
- https://en.wikipedia.org/wiki/IBM_7090#IBM_7094
- https://en.wikipedia.org/wiki/ETA10
- https://en.wikipedia.org/wiki/Intel_Paragon
- https://www.top500.org/featured/systems/asci-red-sandia-national-laboratory/
- https://en.wikipedia.org/wiki/Earth_Simulator
- https://en.wikipedia.org/wiki/Blue_Gene
- https://www.youtube.com/watch?v=OU68MstXsrI

Pacheco, P. S. Parallel Programming with MPI, San Francisco: University of San Francesco, California: Morgan Kaufmann Publishers (1997).

Summary

In this chapter, we learned about John von Neumann's stored-program computer architecture, and its subsequent implementation in physical processors and chips. We also learned how supercomputers are classified using Flynn's classical taxonomy, depending on how the instruction and data stream are implemented in the final design. A historical perspective was provided to contextualize the genesis of supercomputers, and the current quest for even greater supercomputing power. We learned the mechanics behind serial processing and parallel processing, and why parallel processing is more efficient at solving complex problems – if the problem can be logically paralyzed employing MPI. We justified the need for greater processing speed by providing several examples of real-world scenarios such as auto assembly, jet construction, drive-thru lunch, rush hour traffic, plate tectonics, and weather, to list a few examples. Finally, an additional analytical perspective was provided to buttress the need for greater processing speed.

2
One Node Supercomputing

This chapter discusses one node supercomputing. Initially, you will install the Linux (Ubuntu) OS on your PC (one node). Next, you will be instructed on how to access your PC processor's specs within the Windows environment. This information is critical for determining how many cores and/or threads (see Appendix) are available for **Message Passing Interface** (**MPI**) processing when using the -H command (this command is discussed in detail later in the book). You will then write and run a simple serial π equation code, and then write and run the MPI version of the serial π code. This coding exercise provides an initial feel for converting serial coding to MPI coding. The critical structure of the MPI π code's for statement is discussed, and finally, you will employ the MPI technique to generate π from the Euler, Leibniz, and Nilakantha infinite series expansions.

In this chapter, you will learn about the following topics:

- How to install Linux (Ubuntu) on your PC
- The microprocessor in modern PCs
- How to access the technical details of the processor on your PC
- How to write, and run a simple serial π code
- The general structure of MPI
- How to write and run a basic MPI code to call on the cores/processes in the multi-core processor in your PC
- How to write (using the call-processor algorithm) and run a MPI π code version of the previously mentioned serial π code
- The critical structure of the MPI π code involving the for loop statement
- How to write an MPI program to run/generate π from the Euler infinite series
- How to write an MPI program to run/generate π from the Leibniz infinite series
- How to write an MPI program to run/generate π from the Nilakantha infinite series

Linux installation

Before we embark on our digital odyssey, the reader is advised to install the Linux OS on their main PC as we will be using command-line instructions to communicate remotely with your Pi2 or Pi3, via **Secure Shell (SSH)** protocol (more on this later). You may visit the Ubuntu website: `http://www.ubuntu.com/download/desktop/install-ubuntu-desktop` for tutorial/instructions, and download a free version of the OS. In addition, when installing Ubuntu, select the option that allows you to access the Windows OS as you also will eventually be using Windows apps such as win32 Disk imager, and an SD card formatter (we will discuss their download and applications later when you begin configuring your eight-node Pi2 or Pi3 super cluster).

PC processor

The processor in modern PCs has multiple cores. Earlier PC models had two cores, but later PCs typically have four cores, each running at GHz speeds, thus making it possible for you to test/debug the same MPI programs you will be running on your eight-node, 32-core Pi supercomputer. Initially, you will utilize the CPU in your main PC as a one node supercomputer. This step will give you a quick introduction to and demonstration of the MPI protocol. Incidentally, the author's PC has an i7, four-core processor, each core running at 4 GHz, and can run two processing threads per physical core. The initial MPI runs included in this book were done using this 4 GHz machine.

Accessing processor technical details

You can access the technical details of your processor via the **Control Panel** on your computer. On a Windows 7 machine, click on **Systems & Security**, then click on **System**, then **Device Manager**, and click on **Processor**. On the other hand, if you have a Windows 10 OS, proceed as follows. Click on the Windows icon at the bottom left of the taskbar, and then click on the **File Explorer** icon, then click on the **This PC** icon. Next, click on the **Computer** tab at the top left of the displayed window, then click on **System properties**. Note the information displayed in the window. Next, click on **Device Manager**, and then click on **Processors**. You should now see the total number of processors/compute threads in the cores in your PC.

Write/run serial π code

Using your PC as a one-node supercomputer is quite easy, and can be quite a fun exercise as you command the cores in the processor to do your digital bidding. From here on, it will be assumed that the reader has a working knowledge of the C language. So, the first step on your digital journey will be to write and run a simple C code to compute π. This code will perform numeric integration (using 300,000 iterations) on an x function representation of π. You will then convert this code's logic into its MPI version, run it on one core of the processor, and then gradually bring online the remaining cores. You will observe progressively improving processing speed as you activate successive cores. Let's start with the simple π equation:

$$\pi = \int_0^1 \frac{4}{1+x^2}\, dx$$

This equation is one of many that are available for obtaining an approximate value of π. In later sections, we will explore a few more complex and famous equations that will give your supercomputer a more rigorous digital workout. The following code is the requisite serial C code representation of the equation depicted previously:

```
C_PI.c:

#include <math.h> // math library
#include <stdio.h>// Standard Input/Output library

int main(void)
{
  long num_rects = 300000;//1000000000;
  long i;
  double x,height,width,area;
  double sum;
  width = 1.0/(double)num_rects; // width of a segment

  sum = 0;
  for(i = 0; i < num_rects; i++)
  {
    x = (i+0.5) * width; // x: distance to center of
    i(th) segment
    height = 4/(1.0 + x*x);
    sum += height; // sum of individual segment heights
  }

// approximate area of segment (Pi value)
  area = width * sum;
```

```
    printf("n");
    printf(" Calculated Pi = %.16fn", area);
    printf("          M_PI = %.16fn", M_PI);
    printf("Relative error = %.16fn", fabs(area - M_PI));

    return 0;
}
```

This code was written using the vim editor in the Linux terminal environment (click on the **black monitor** icon to open the terminal window). First, change the directory to the Desktop folder by entering the command cd Desktop. Now create a blank C filename C_PI.c (feel free to name your code anything you desire within the terminal window) by entering the command vim C_PI.c. Press *i* to initiate editing. Type or copy in the code as shown previously. Save the file by entering Esc :wq, which returns you to the $ prompt.

You remain in the Desktop directory. Compile the code using the mpicc C_PI.c -o C_PI command. This procedure generates an executable filename C_PI located in the Desktop folder.

Finally, run the code using the time mpiexec C_PI command. The code will generate the output depicted in the following run. You may see four similar outputs, each emanating from a core in the four-core processor:

```
carlospg@gamma:~/Desktop/Master_Pi2$ time mpiexec C_PI

 Calculated Pi = 3.1415926535906125
          M_PI = 3.1415926535897931
Relative error = 0.0000000000008193


real    0m0.039s
user    0m0.036s
sys     0m0.000s
```

Feel free to modify the code by changing the value of num_rects (whose current value is 300,000), and observe the change in the accuracy of the calculation. The code's calculation time should change accordingly. Note that this calculation ran on only one core. The calculation or task was not shared/divided among the four cores. The run time of (0m0.039s), highlighted in red, is a function of the relatively fast 4 GHz processor. Your processor may have a slower speed, and hence the computation time may be somewhat elevated. We now proceed to that much vaunted MPI protocol.

Message passing interface

The general structure of MPI programs is depicted here (please visit the links provided in the introduction for a more in-depth discussion on the topic). Your MPI codes will have elements of this structure:

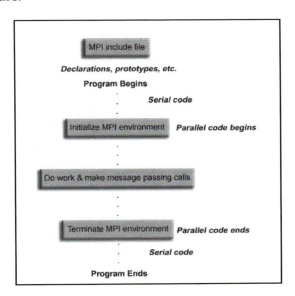

Basic MPI code

A relatively simple MPI code is shown here. You will notice how the code mirrors the general structure of MPI programs:

```
call-procs.c:
#include <math.h> // math library
#include <stdio.h>// Standard Input/Output library

int main(int argc, char** argv)
{
  /* MPI Variables */
  int num_processes;
  int curr_rank;
  int proc_name_len;
  char proc_name[MPI_MAX_PROCESSOR_NAME];

  /* Initialize MPI */
```

```
    MPI_Init (&argc, &argv);

    /* acquire number of processes */
    MPI_Comm_size(MPI_COMM_WORLD, &num_processes);

    /* acquire rank of the current process */
    MPI_Comm_rank(MPI_COMM_WORLD, &curr_rank);

    /* acquire processor name for the current thread */
    MPI_Get_processor_name(proc_name, &proc_name_len);

    /* output rank, no of processes, and process name */
    printf("Calling process %d out of %d on %srn",
    curr_rank, num_processes,
    proc_name);

    /* clean up, done with MPI */
    MPI_Finalize();

    return 0;
}
```

Your typical MPI code must contain, in large part, as the statements highlighted. There are however, many more statements/functions available for use, depending on the task you want to accomplish. We will not concern ourselves with those other statements, except for the following statements/functions:

```
"MPI_Bcast(&n, 1, MPI_INT, 0, MPI_COMM_WORLD);" and
"MPI_Reduce(&rank_integral,&pi, 1, MPI_DOUBLE,
 MPI_SUM, 0, MPI_COMM_WORLD);",
```

You will add these to the π version of the code. The basic MPI code depicted previously was given the filename call-procs.c. Compile the code using the mpicc call-procs.c -o call-procs command. Run it using the mpiexec -n 8 call-procs command; the -n designates n threads or processes, followed by the number 8 – the number of threads or processes you want to use in the calculation. The result is shown here. Here, the author is using all eight threads in the four cores in his PC processor. The code randomly calls on the various processes, out of a total of 8, on the host computer gamma on which the code is running:

```
carlospg@gamma:~/Desktop/Master_Pi2$ mpiexec -n 8 call-procs
Calling process 0 out of 8 on gamma
Calling process 1 out of 8 on gamma
Calling process 2 out of 8 on gamma
Calling process 5 out of 8 on gamma
Calling process 7 out of 8 on gamma
Calling process 3 out of 8 on gamma
Calling process 4 out of 8 on gamma
Calling process 6 out of 8 on gamma
```

MPI π code

The MPI π code (filename `MPI_08_b.c`), with its run, is depicted on the following pages:

```
MPI_08_b.c:
#include <mpi.h>  // (Open)MPI library
#include <math.h> // math library
#include <stdio.h>// Standard Input/Output library

int main(int argc, char*argv[])
{
  int total_iter;
  int n, rank, length, numprocs, i;
  double pi, width, sum, x, rank_integral;
  char hostname[MPI_MAX_PROCESSOR_NAME];
  MPI_Init(&argc, &argv);// initiates MPI
  MPI_Comm_size(MPI_COMM_WORLD, &numprocs);// acquire
  number of processes
  MPI_Comm_rank(MPI_COMM_WORLD, &rank);// acquire current
  process id
  MPI_Get_processor_name(hostname, &length);// acquire
  hostname

  if(rank == 0)
  {
    printf("n");
 printf("########################################################");
    printf("nn");
    printf("Master node name: %sn", hostname);
    printf("n");
    printf("Enter the number of intervals:n");
    printf("n");
    scanf("%d",&n);
    printf("n");
  }
```

```
// broadcast to all processes, the number of segments you
want
MPI_Bcast(&n, 1, MPI_INT, 0, MPI_COMM_WORLD);

// this loop increments the maximum number of iterations, thus providing
// additional work for testing computational speed of the processors
for(total_iter = 1; total_iter < n; total_iter++)
{
   sum=0.0;
   width = 1.0 / (double)total_iter; // width of a segment
   // width = 1.0 / (double)n; // width of a segment
   for(i = rank + 1; i <= total_iter; i += numprocs)
   // for(i = rank + 1; i <= n; i += numprocs)
   {
      x = width * ((double)i - 0.5); // x: distance to
      center of i(th) segment
      sum += 4.0/(1.0 + x*x);// sum of individual segment
      height for a given
                           // rank
   }
// approximate area of segment (Pi value) for a given rank
   rank_integral = width * sum;

// collect and add the partial area (Pi) values from all processes
   MPI_Reduce(&rank_integral, &pi, 1, MPI_DOUBLE, MPI_SUM,
   0, MPI_COMM_WORLD);
}// End of for(total_iter = 1; total_iter < n; total_iter++)

if(rank == 0)
{
   printf("nn");
   printf("*** Number of processes: %dn",numprocs);
   printf("nn");
   printf("      Calculated pi = %.30fn", pi);
   printf("              M_PI = %.30fn", M_PI);
   printf("     Relative Error = %.30fn", fabs(pi-M_PI));
   // printf("Process %d on %s has the partial result of
   %.16f n",rank,hostname,
   rank_integral);
}

// clean up, done with MPI
MPI_Finalize();

return 0;
}// End of int main(int argc, char*argv[])
```

Compile and run this MPI C code. The result is depicted following. Notice the `time` parameter used for displaying the execution time beneath the program result. You will notice the gradual reduction in execution time as successively more processes/threads are brought online:

```
carlospg@gamma:~/Desktop/Master_Pi2$ time mpiexec -n 8 MPI_0(

##########################################################

Master node name: gamma

Enter the number of intervals:

300000


*** Number of processes: 8


        Calculated pi = 3.1415926535907150
               M_PI = 3.1415926535897931
        Relative Error = 0.0000000000009219

real    0m59.076s
user    5m2.672s
sys     1m25.868s
```

Critical MPI for loop structure

We will now discuss the most critical structure of the MPI version of the serial π code – the `for (i = rank + 1; i <= total_iter; i += numprocs)` statement. This construct assigns the data among the various processes. The variable `numprocs` has the value 8 – the author chose all eight threads (two per core) to do his digital bidding. So, for the eight processes/ranks, that is, 0, 1, 2, 3, 4, 5, 6, 7, and the ith segment (total 300,000) of the area under the π function curve, is assigned as follows:

Rank	Loop 1	Loop 2	Loop 3	Loop 4	Loop 5	Loop 6	Loop 7	Loop 8	Loop 9
0	1	9	17	25	33	41	49	57	65
1	2	10	18	26	34	42	50	58	66
2	3	11	19	27	35	43	51	59	67
3	4	12	20	28	36	44	52	60	68
4	5	13	21	29	37	45	53	61	69
5	6	14	22	30	38	46	54	62	70
6	7	15	23	31	39	47	55	63	71
7	8	16	24	32	40	48	56	64	72

Rank 0 is assigned the 1st, 9th, 17th, 25th, 33rd, 41st, 49th, 57th, 65th, and so on segments; rank 1 is assigned the 2nd, 10th, 18th, 26th, 34th, 42nd, 50th, 58th, 66th, and so on segments; and so on and so forth. This table extends to the 300,000th iteration/loop. So, for each rank, the distance x to the center of the ith segment as follows: width of a segment *(width)* $\times (i^{th} - 0.5)$. This x value is now used to calculate the height of the ith segment within its rank or processor core. The calculated heights for a given rank are continuously summed *(sum += 4.0 / (1.0+x*x))* with each iteration/loop, and stored in that process temporary memory. Note that even though the `sum` variable is used by each process, it is a unique memory location for that process, so the data from one process will not contaminate the data in another process within a core, even though the processes use the same variable name. The author appreciates how perplexing this may seem to you; however, as they say in street parlance, that's how MPI rolls. After the 300,000th iteration/loop, the partial sum from each process/core is then combined/summed by the `MPI_Reduce` function to give the overall value for π. Note that we ask the 0 rank or process to print/display the result. This is standard operating procedure.

With regards to the outer `for` loop, it is used to extend the computational time for the simple pi calculation – the astute reader would have noticed that the computational time for one core, using the MPI protocol, is slower than the serial code using the same core; that is, 2m37.693s, as opposed to `0m0.039s`. This occurs because the outer for loop incrementally increases the value of the upper limit `total_iter` – the maximum number of iterations – as the code executes. This intentional increase in processing time is to aid in making any improvement in the computational time compression perceptible, as you successively add more cores. Otherwise, for this simple π calculation, computation would be over in a very short time when using the maximum number of cores – not much fun if you are a novice in supercomputing – you want to observe your eventual newly minted Pi2 or Pi3 supercomputer producing digital sweat by working hard. You can always remove this artificial limitation (restrained mode) when you desire maximum computing power while performing legitimate work. Feel free to experiment by commenting out the outer `for` statement and replacing the inner `for` statement with `for (i = rank + 1; i <= n; i += numprocs)`, where the value of n is the maximum number of iterations you entered at the initial run of the code (don't forget to also comment out `width = 1.0/(double)total_itar`, while uncommenting the statement immediately following). You should now notice a substantial drop in computational time for π.

Note how the run time shrinks with the activation of additional threads, processes, and cores. We now have undisputed evidence of the advantages of parallel processing. Be audacious, and improve your coding skills by modifying your codes, or writing new codes with other MPI functions listed on the websites provided in the introduction.

Now that you've had a taste of running MPI, lets now write and run three more exotic π equations that were discovered by the famous mathematicians Euler, Leibniz, and Nilakantha. Let's tackle first the Euler (Swiss mathematician, physicist, astronomer, logician, and engineer) equation:

$$\frac{\pi^2}{6} = \sum_{k=1}^{\infty} \frac{1}{k^2}$$

$$\pi = \sqrt[2]{\sum_{k=1}^{\infty} \frac{6}{k^2}}$$

Copy or create the file using the; `vim Euler.c` command. Compile the file using `mpicc Euler.c -o Euler -lm`. The `-lm` links the math library header, `<math.h>`. Run the program using; `time mpiexec -n x Euler`, where x is replaced by the number of threads/cores you want to employ.

MPI Euler code

Here is the code for Euler:

```
Euler.c:
#include <mpi.h>  // (Open)MPI library
#include <math.h> // math library
#include <stdio.h>// Standard Input/Output library

int main(int argc, char*argv[])
{
  int total_iter;
  int n,rank,length,numprocs,i;
  double sum,sum0,rank_integral,A;
  char hostname[MPI_MAX_PROCESSOR_NAME];

  MPI_Init(&argc, &argv);// initiates MPI
  MPI_Comm_size(MPI_COMM_WORLD, &numprocs); // acquire
  number of processes
```

```
MPI_Comm_rank(MPI_COMM_WORLD, &rank);      // acquire
current process id
MPI_Get_processor_name(hostname, &length);// acquire
hostname

if(rank == 0)
{
  printf("n");
  printf("########################################################");
  printf("nn");
  printf("Master node name: %sn", hostname);
  printf("n");
  printf("Enter the number of intervals:n");
  printf("n");
  scanf("%d",&n);
  printf("n");
}

// broadcast the number of iterations "n" in the
infinite series
MPI_Bcast(&n, 1, MPI_INT, 0, MPI_COMM_WORLD);

// this loop increments the maximum number of
iterations, thus providing
// additional work for testing computational speed of
the processors
for(total_iter = 1; total_iter < n; total_iter++)
{
  sum0 = 0.0;
  for(i = rank + 1; i <= total_iter; i += numprocs)
  {
    A = 1.0/(double)pow(i,2);
    sum0 += A;
  }

  rank_integral = sum0;// Partial sum for a given rank

  // collect and add the partial sum0 values from all
  processes
  MPI_Reduce(&rank_integral, &sum, 1, MPI_DOUBLE,
  MPI_SUM, 0,
  MPI_COMM_WORLD);

} // End of for(total_iter = 1; total_iter < n;
total_iter++)

if(rank == 0)
{
```

```
    printf("nn");
    printf("*** Number of processes: %dn",numprocs);
    printf("nn");
    printf("    Calculated pi = %.30fn", sqrt(6*sum));
    printf("             M_PI = %.30fn", M_PI);
    printf("    Relative Error = %.30fn",
    fabs(sqrt(6*sum)-M_PI));
}

// clean up, done with MPI
MPI_Finalize();

return 0;
}// End of int main(int argc, char*argv[])
```

Let's check out the code run for Euler now:

```
carlospg@gamma:~/Desktop$ time mpiexec -n 1 Euler

#######################################################

Master node name: gamma

Enter the number of intervals:

300000


*** Number of processes: 1


    Calculated pi = 3.141589470484041246578499340103
             M_PI = 3.141592653589793115997963468544
    Relative Error = 0.000003183105751869419464128441

Real  3m51.168s
user  3m45.792s
sys   0m0.012s


carlospg@gamma:~/Desktop$ time mpiexec -n 2 Euler

#######################################################

Master node name: gamma

Enter the number of intervals:
```

```
300000

*** Number of processes: 2

    Calculated pi = 3.14158947048406611557425094 3610
            M_PI = 3.141592653589793115997963468544
   Relative Error = 0.0000031831057270004237125249 35

real   2m0.190s
user   3m55.128s
sys    0m0.020s


carlospg@gamma:~/Desktop$ time mpiexec -n 3 Euler

#######################################################

Master node name: gamma

Enter the number of intervals:

300000


*** Number of processes: 3


    Calculated pi = 3.141589470484025703456154587911
            M_PI = 3.141592653589793115997963468544
   Relative Error = 0.0000031831057674125418088806 33

real   1m32.108s
user   4m27.736s
sys    0m0.016s


carlospg@gamma:~/Desktop$ time mpiexec -n 4 Euler

#######################################################

Master node name: gamma

Enter the number of intervals:

300000


*** Number of processes: 4
```

```
Calculated pi = 3.1415894704840470197382227390917
         M_PI = 3.1415926535897931159979634685441
Relative Error = 0.00000318310574609625973607762741
```

```
real    1m14.463s
user    4m51.544s
sys     0m0.040s
```

 The execution time drops as we bring more cores online.

Let's write and run Leibniz (German polymath, inventor of differential and integral calculus along with Sir Isaac Newton, and philosopher):

$$\frac{\pi}{4} = \frac{1}{3} + \frac{1}{5} - \frac{1}{7} + \frac{1}{9} - \cdots$$

$$\pi = \sum_{k=0}^{\infty} (-1)^k \frac{4}{2k+1}$$

Copy or create the file using the command; vim Leibniz.c. Compile the file using; mpicc Leibniz.c -o Leibniz -lm. The -lm links the math library header <math.h>. Run the program using the command; time mpiexec -n x Leibniz, where x is replaced by the number of threads/cores you want to employ.

MPI Leibniz code

The Gregory-Leibniz code is follows:

```
Leibniz.c:
#include <mpi.h>  // (Open)MPI library
#include <math.h> // math library
#include <stdio.h>// Standard Input/Output library

int main(int argc, char*argv[])
{
  int total_iter;
  int n, rank,length,numprocs;
  double rank_sum,pi,sum,A;
  unsignedlong i,k;
```

```
char hostname[MPI_MAX_PROCESSOR_NAME];

MPI_Init(&argc, &argv); // initiates MPI
MPI_Comm_size(MPI_COMM_WORLD, &numprocs); // acquire number of processes
MPI_Comm_rank(MPI_COMM_WORLD, &rank);      // acquire current process id
MPI_Get_processor_name(hostname, &length);// acquire hostname

if (rank == 0)
{
  printf("n");
  printf("######################################################");
  printf("nn");
  printf("Master node name: %sn", hostname);
  printf("n");
  printf("Enter the number of intervals:n");
  printf("n");
  scanf("%d",&n);
  printf("n");
}

// broadcast the number of iterations "n" in the infinite series
MPI_Bcast(&n, 1, MPI_INT, 0, MPI_COMM_WORLD);

// this loop increments the maximum number of iterations, thus providing
// additional work for testing computational speed of the processors

for(total_iter = 1; total_iter < n; total_iter++)
{
  sum = 0.0;
  for(i = rank + 1; i <= total_iter; i += numprocs)
  {
    k = i-1;
    A = (double)pow(-1,k)* 4.0/(double)(2*k+1);

    sum += A;
  }

  rank_sum = sum;// Partial sum for a given rank

  // collect and add the partial sum values from all
  processes
  MPI_Reduce(&rank_sum, &pi, 1, MPI_DOUBLE, MPI_SUM, 0,
 MPI_COMM_WORLD);

} // End of for(total_iter = 1; total_iter < n;
total_iter++)

if(rank == 0)
```

```
{
    printf("nn");
    printf("*** Number of processes: %dn",numprocs);
    printf("nn");
    printf("     Calculated pi = %.30fn", pi);
    printf("             M_PI = %.30fn", M_PI);
    printf("    Relative Error = %.30fn", fabs(pi-M_PI));
}

// clean up, done with MPI
MPI_Finalize();

return 0;
}
```

Now, let's go through the code run for Gregory-Leibniz:

```
carlospg@gamma:~/Desktop$ time mpiexec -n 1 Gregory_Leibniz

###################################################

Master node name: gamma

Enter the number of intervals:

300000


*** Number of processes: 1

    Calculated pi = 3.141595986934242024091190614854
            M_PI = 3.141592653589793115997963468544
   Relative Error = 0.000003333344448908093227146310

real    25m13.914s
user    25m8.500s
sys     0m0.012s


carlospg@gamma:~/Desktop$ time mpiexec -n 2 Gregory_Leibniz

###################################################

Master node name: gamma

Enter the number of intervals:

300000
```

```
*** Number of processes: 2


    Calculated pi = 3.14159598693365893494958657482639
            M_PI = 3.14159265358979311599796346844
   Relative Error = 0.00000333343865818960694014095

real   13m5.893s
user   26m5.500s
sys    0m0.052s



carlospg@gamma:~/Desktop$ time mpiexec -n 3 Gregory_Leibniz

###########################################################

Master node name: gamma

Enter the number of intervals:

300000


*** Number of processes: 3


    Calculated pi = 3.14159598693420205606230410921
            M_PI = 3.14159265358979311599796346844
   Relative Error = 0.0000033333444089400643406406744

real   8m57.444s
user   26m46.880s
sys    0m0.040s



carlospg@gamma:~/Desktop$ time mpiexec -n 4 Gregory_Leibniz

###########################################################

Master node name: gamma

Enter the number of intervals:

300000


*** Number of processes: 4
```

```
   Calculated pi = 3.1415959869343215160597 53776062
            M_PI = 3.1415926535897931159979 63468544
  Relative Error = 0.0000033333445284000617 90307518

real   7m14.118s
user   28m31.732s
sys    0m0.116s
```

The execution time drops as we bring more cores online.

Let's now write and run Nilakantha (brilliant Indian mathematician and astronomer):

$$\pi = 3 + \frac{4}{2 \times 3 \times 4} - \frac{4}{4 \times 5 \times 6} + \frac{4}{6 \times 7 \times 8} - \frac{4}{8 \times 9 \times 10} + \cdots$$

$$\pi = 3 + \sum_{k=0}^{\infty} (-1)^{(k+2)} \left(\frac{4}{(2k+2)(2k+3)(2k+4)} \right)$$

Copy or create the file using; `vim Nilakantha.c` command. Compile the file using `mpicc Nilakantha.c -o Nilakantha -lm`. The `-lm` links the math library header, `math.h`. Run the program using; `time mpiexec -n x Nilakantha`, where x is replaced by the number of threads/cores you want to employ.

MPI Nilakantha code

The code for Nilakantha is given as follows:

```
Nilakantha.c:
#include <mpi.h>  // (Open)MPI library
#include <math.h> // math library
#include <stdio.h>// Standard Input/Output library

int main(int argc, char*argv[])
{
  int total_iter;
  int n,rank,length,numprocs,i,k;
  double sum,sum0,rank_integral,A,B,C;
  char hostname[MPI_MAX_PROCESSOR_NAME];

  MPI_Init(&argc, &argv);// initiates MPI
```

```
MPI_Comm_size(MPI_COMM_WORLD, &numprocs); // acquire number of processes
MPI_Comm_rank(MPI_COMM_WORLD, &rank);     // acquire current process id
MPI_Get_processor_name(hostname, &length);// acquire hostname

if(rank == 0)
{
   printf("n");
   printf("############################################################");
   printf("nn");
   printf("Master node name: %sn", hostname);
   printf("n");
   printf("Enter the number of intervals:n");
   printf("n");
   scanf("%d",&n);
   printf("n");
}

// broadcast to all processes, the number of segments you want
MPI_Bcast(&n, 1, MPI_INT, 0, MPI_COMM_WORLD);

// this loop increments the maximum number of iterations, thus providing
// additional work for testing computational speed of the processors
for(total_iter = 1; total_iter < n; total_iter++)
{
   sum0 = 0.0;
   for(i = rank + 1; i <= total_iter; i += numprocs)
   {
      k = i-1;
      A = (double)pow(-1,k+2);
      B = 4.0/(double)((k+1)*(k+2)*(k+3));
      C = A * B;

      sum0 += C;
   }

   rank_integral = sum0;// Partial sum for a given rank

   // collect and add the partial sum0 values from all processes
   MPI_Reduce(&rank_integral, &sum, 1, MPI_DOUBLE, MPI_SUM, 0,
   MPI_COMM_WORLD);

} // End of for(total_iter = 1; total_iter < n; total_iter++)

if(rank == 0)
{
   printf("nn");
   printf("*** Number of processes: %dn",numprocs);
   printf("nn");
```

```
    printf("      Calculated pi = %.30fn", (3+sum));
    printf("              M_PI = %.30fn", M_PI);
    printf("     Relative Error = %.30fn", fabs((3+sum)-M_PI));
}
// clean up, done with MPI
MPI_Finalize();

return 0;
}// End of int main(int argc, char*argv[])
```

Let's have a look at the code run for Nilakantha;

```
carlospg@gamma:~/Desktop$ time mpiexec -n 1 Nilakantha

########################################################

Master node name: gamma

Enter the number of intervals:

300000


*** Number of processes: 1


    Calculated pi = 3.141448792732286499074234598083
            M_PI = 3.141592653589793115997963468544
   Relative Error = 0.000143860857506616923728870461

real   24m37.130s
user   24m31.772s
sys    0m0.008s


carlospg@gamma:~/Desktop$ time mpiexec -n 2 Nilakantha

########################################################

Master node name: gamma
Enter the number of intervals:

300000


*** Number of processes: 2
```

```
    Calculated pi = 3.14144879273229093996633309870
           M_PI = 3.14159265358979311599796346854
  Relative Error = 0.00014386085750217603163036983

real  12m36.831s
user  25m6.088s
sys   0m0.008s

carlospg@gamma:~/Desktop$ time mpiexec -n 3 Nilakantha

#######################################################

Master node name: gamma

Enter the number of intervals:

300000


*** Number of processes: 3

    Calculated pi = 3.14144879273229005178791339858
           M_PI = 3.14159265358979311599796346854
  Relative Error = 0.00014386085750306421005006996

real  9m0.872s
user  26m30.512s
sys   0m0.052s


carlospg@gamma:~/Desktop$ time mpiexec -n 4 Nilakantha

#######################################################

Master node name: gamma

Enter the number of intervals:

300000


*** Number of processes: 4

    Calculated pi = 3.14144879273228827543107399833
           M_PI = 3.14159265358979311599796346854
  Relative Error = 0.00014386085750484056688947021
```

```
real   6m56.071s
user   27m10.824s
sys    0m0.052s
```

 The execution time drops as we bring more cores online. A 4 GHz processor generated the preceding run times. It is quite likely that your run times will be different from that of the author's, depending on your processor speed.

Now that you have sampled the extreme power that awaits you at your beck and call, let's now proceed to build that much anticipated Pi2 or Pi3 supercomputer.

Summary

In this chapter, we learned how to download and install Ubuntu on the main PC. We wrote and ran a simple serial π code on one core of your PC multi-core processor, and then wrote and ran the first MPI code to call on the cores/processes in the multi-core processor in your PC. Armed with this knowledge/technique, we wrote and ran the MPI code version of the simple serial π code, and in the process learned how the `for` loop distributes the work/task among the cores in the processor for attaining an ultimate solution. Finally, we employed the MPI coding technique learned to generate the π values from the Euler, Leibniz, and Nilakantha infinite series. In Chapter 3, *Preparing the Initial Two Nodes*, we will learn how to prepare the initial two nodes of your Pi2 or Pi3 supercomputer.

3
Preparing the Initial Two Nodes

Building a multi-node Pi2 or Pi3 supercomputer requires configuring, initially, the first two nodes (master and first slave). The slave1 disk image (more on this later) can then be cloned for producing any number of remaining slave nodes, as you expand the processing capacity of the super stack. In the ensuing paragraphs, you will be presented with a list of parts. You will learn about the origin of the Pi microcomputer and its technical specs. Additionally, you will be instructed on how to configure the master Pi node, in preparation for transferring the requisite test codes from the main PC to the master node, and finally, you will configure the first slave node to create a two-node supercomputer.

In this chapter, you will learn about the following topics:

- The list of parts required for the Pi2 or Pi3 supercomputer
- The origin of the Pi microcomputer
- The critical specs of the Pi processor
- How to configure the master node
- How to transfer the requisite codes to the master node from the main PC
- How to configure the first slave node of the two-node Pi2 or Pi3 supercomputer

Listing of parts

You may acquire all or part of your supplies from Amazon, Adafruit, or any other online hobby or electronic parts stores. However, the author built his supercomputer from parts acquired exclusively from Amazon.

The following is a list of things you will need to build your supercomputer:

- Eight Raspberry Pi2 or Pi3 model B computers -> *8 x $39.99 = $319.92.*
- Addicore Raspberry Pi heatsink set of three aluminum heat sinks -> *8 x $4.95 = $39.60.*
- Eight-pack, eight-color (3 feet long) Ethernet patch cables from cable matters -> *1 x $12.99 = $12.99.*
- Extra Ethernet patch cable for connection to the main PC.
- Eight 16-GB SD cards from SanDisk or other, preloaded with NOOBS (optional, can download from website). Purchase a 10-pack and save -> *1 x $49.43 = $49.43.*
- Four sets of stackable case (sidewinder) for Raspberry Pi2 model B from HDZ concepts -> *4 x $15.98 = $63.92.*
- One Sabrent 60-watt (12-amp) 10-port family-sized desktop USB rapid charger -> *1 x $37.99 = $37.99.*
- Eight Sabrent 22AWG premium 3ft micro USB cables; you might have to purchase a six-pack and a three-pack -> *1 x $9.99 = $9.99.*
- One wireless Edimax EW-7811Un 150Mbps 11n Wi-Fi USB adapter -> *1 x $8.99 = $8.99.*
- One HPE networking BTO JG536A#ABA 1910-8 managed switch -> *1 x $85.99 = $85.99.*
- One extended Ethernet cable to connect to your router if it is not close to your work area. The author had to purchase a 50-ft-long cable to reach his workstation -> *1 x $9.49 = $9.49.*
- One HI definition monitor with HDMI connector for connecting to the Raspberry Pi2 board, for example, Sunfounder 7'HD 1024*600 TFT LCD screen display -> *1 x $59.99 = $59.99.*
- One C2G/cables to go 43036 4-inch cable ties – 100 pack (black) -> *1 x $3.07 = $3.07.*
- One Amazon basics high-speed HDMI cable – 3 feet (latest standard) -> *1 x $4.99 = $4.99.*
- One Rii Mini K12 keyboard, Fig. 42, or alternatively, one Anker CB310 full-size ergonomic wireless keyboard and mouse combo -> *1 x $39.99 = $39.99.*

The Pi2/Pi3 computer

The Raspberry Pi2 model B (see the following figure) has a few siblings. Some are less capable than the Pi2, and others, such as the newer Pi3, have greater capability in terms of processing power. However, in the following endeavor, the author used the Pi2, even though he could have used the Pi3 (the Pi3 is discussed in the latter sections of `Chapter 8`, *Testing the Super Cluster*). The Pi technology was invented in the United Kingdom in February 2012. The device is the progeny of an idea – conceived at the Raspberry Pi foundation – that places of learning around the UK should be equipped to teach individuals the basics of computer science. The low-cost technology quickly gained popularity in England, and subsequently in the US. Contributing affirmatively to the device's rapid acceptance is its use of an opensource Linux-based operating system. The Linux OS is a boon to tech geeks around the world, who are now using this Pi microcomputer in ways that were never imagined by its developers, such as the supercomputer that you will be constructing shortly. You may visit the Raspberry <ie>Pi</ie> website, `https://www.raspberrypi.org`, to see a myriad of other ways in which this capable little device can be used. Additional technical details about the Pi2 may also be gleaned from the Adafruit links `https://cdn-shop.adafruit.com/pdfs/raspberrypi2modelb.pdf` and `https://cdn-learn.adafruit.com/downloads/pdf/introducing-the-raspberry-pi-2-model-b.pdf`, and the Pi organization website, `https://www.raspberrypi.org/products/raspberry-pi-2-model-b/`.

The following figure depicts the top view of the Raspberry Pi2 showing the aluminum cooling fins affixed to the Ethernet controller microchip, and the larger broadcom **Central Processing Unit (CPU)** microchip:

Raspberry Pi2 model B, top view

The following figure depicts the bottom view of the Raspberry Pi2; note the SD card in its holder/slot located at the center-left of the PC board, and the RAM chip (square black component) located at the approximate center of the board:

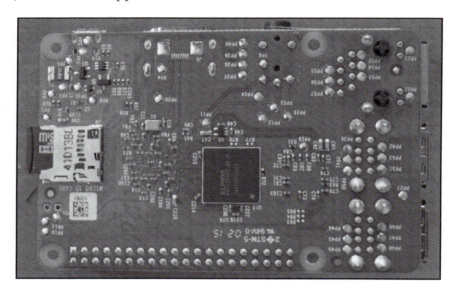

Raspberry Pi2 model B, bottom view

The Pi2 B has a four-core CPU, capable of running one processing thread per core, and 1 GB of **Random Access Memory (RAM)**, located approximately at the center of the bottom of the board. Each CPU core operates at 900 MHz clock speed, that is, the processor executes at 900,000,000 **Cycles Per Second (CPS)** (the relationship between CPS and **Floating Point Operations Per Second (FLOPS)** can be gleaned from the websites https://en.wikipedia.org/wiki/FLOPS and https://www.quora.com/How-do-you-convert-GHz-to-FLOPS). Nevertheless, you can overclock the Pi2 (not the Pi3, its clock speed is fixed at 1.2 GHz) to operate at 1 GHz (you will be instructed on how to accomplish this speed upgrade later). This higher overclocked processing speed will produce an elevated temperature within the CPU. You can, however, mitigate this heating issue by simply attaching cooling fins to the surface of the chips, and thereby extending the life of the processor. The fins can be purchased from Amazon, Adafruit, or any other online store that sells the Pi boards. It should be noted that, for the pending effort, the more advanced, and slightly less expensive Pi3, https://www.raspberrypi.org/products/raspberry-pi-3-model-b/, could have been substituted for the Pi2.

Project overview

For this project, you will perform the following steps:

1. You will initially configure a Pi2 or Pi3 (one-node), four-core supercomputer.
2. You will then command (using OpenMPI) all four cores to simultaneously solve the simple π equations discussed previously.
3. You will then proceed to assemble a two-node Pi2 or Pi3, 8-core supercomputer, which you will configure to operate in parallel with each other, and again, run said π programs using all eight cores.
4. Finally, you will construct an eight-node Pi2 or Pi3, 32- or 64-core supercomputer, which you will then command to rapidly crunch and smash through substantial equations (see equations in the `Appendix`). Some of these equations require as few as two iterations, while others require hundreds or thousands, and millions of iterations to produce an excellent approximate π value. You will, indeed, be delighted at observing the gradual reduction in processing time, as you successively bring online increasing numbers of cores (1 to 32 or 64) to assist with solving the complex calculations. The following sections discuss the construction and configuration of an eight-node Pi2 or Pi3 supercomputer.

Super stack assembly

Let's have a look at the hardware we would be using to assemble the super cluster. First up are the aluminum cooling fins used to cool the microchips on the Pi computer:

Aluminium cooling fins (eight sets needed)

Next, we see two Pi3s secured in the stackable case as it should appear in your two-node supercomputer. You will expand on this as you build the 8 or 16-node supercomputer:

Sidewinder stackable case with Pi2/3 secured

The following are the figures of the Ethernet color-coded cables that you will be using to connect your cluster to the network switch:

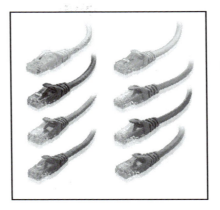

Cable Matters 8-Color Combo, Cat5e Snagless Ethernet Patch Cable 3 Feet.

The following is the Sabrent 60 Watts 10-port USB rapid charger you will be using to power your super cluster:

Sabrent 60 Watts (12 Amp) 10-Port Family-Sized Desktop USB Rapid Charger

The following is the HPE BTO JG536A#ABA1910-8 managed network switch for connecting the nodes in your supercomputer:

HPE Networking BTO JG536A#ABA1910-8 managed switch

The following figure is that of the **Rii** mini K12 stainless steel cover wireless keyboard for use with the super cluster; you may use any other keyboard, if that is your desire:

Rii Mini K12 Stainless Steel Cover Wireless Keyboard with wireless adapter

The following is the figure of the eight-node fully assembled Pi2 or Pi3 supercomputer:

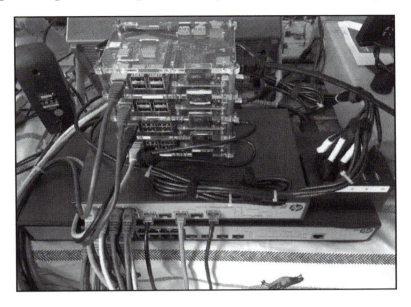

The completely assembled Pi2 or Pi3 super cluster

Carefully unpack and assemble the hardware as depicted in the assembled Pi2 or Pi3 super cluster figure:

1. Install Ubuntu on the main PC with the option to access Windows OS.
2. Affix aluminum cooling fins to the broadcom CPU on all Pi2 or Pi3s.
3. Construct the Pi2 or Pi3 tower. It is pretty straightforward; see the preceding figure.
4. Connect the color-coded Ethernet cables between the eight-input port on the network switch and the Pi2 or Pi3s.
5. Connect the HDMI cable between the designated master Pi2 or Pi3, and the HDMI monitor.
6. Label and connect the eight power micro USB cables to the Pi2 or Pi3s. The socket is on the same side as the HDMI socket. Observe the master Pi2 located at the top-right corner in the preceding tower.
7. Connect only the master Pi2 or Pi3 micro USB cable to the 60 Watts (2 Amp) USB rapid charger.
8. Connect the extra Ethernet cable between the main PC and the network switch (see following `Chapter 4`, *Static IP Address and Hosts File Setup*).

9. Insert an SD card with NOOBS preinstalled into the master Pi2 or Pi3. Label side facing outward.
10. Connect the extended Ethernet cable between the network switch and router (see `Chapter 4`, *Static IP Address and Hosts File Setup*).
11. Power up and plug in the network switch and the rapid charger; only the master Pi2 or Pi3 is energized.
12. Select only the **Raspbian** (see `Appendix`) option and then click **install**. Installation takes several minutes.

Preparing the master node

During bootup, select the US or (whatever country you reside in) keyboard option located at the middle-bottom of the screen. After bootup completes, start with the following screenshot. Click on **Menu**, and then **Preferences**. Select **Raspberry Pi configuration** (see the following screenshot):

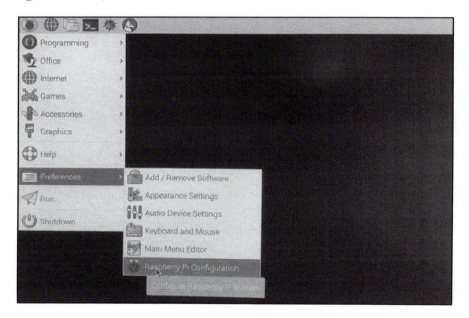

Menu options

The **System** tab appears (see the following screenshot). Type in a suitable **Hostname** for your master Pi. **Auto login** is already checked:

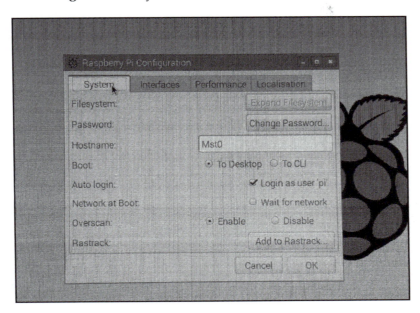

System tab

Go ahead and **Change Password** to your preference (see the following screenshot):

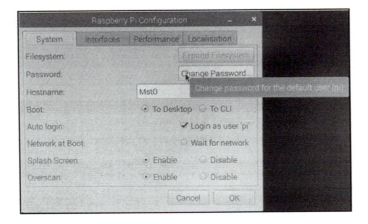

Change password

Select the **Interfaces** tab (see the following screenshot). Click **Enable** on all options, especially **Secure Shell (SSH)**, as you will be remotely logging into the Pi2 or Pi3 from your main PC. The other options are enabled for convenience, as you may be using the Pi2 or Pi3 in other projects outside of supercomputing:

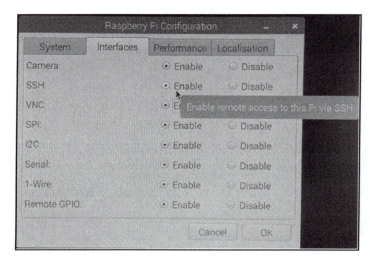

Interface options

The next important step is to boost the processing speed from **900MHz** to 1000 MHz or 1 GHz (this option is only available on the Pi2). Click on the **Performance** tab (see the following screenshot) and select **1000MHz**. You are indeed building a supercomputer, so you need to muster all the available computing muscle. Leave the **GPU Memory** as it is (default). The author used a 32 GB SD card in the master Pi2, hence the **128** MB default setting:

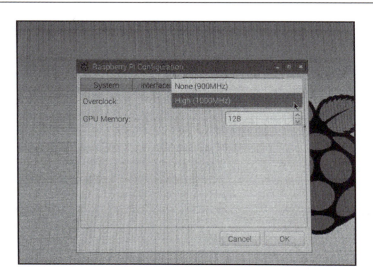

Performance overclock option

Changing the processor clock speed requires reboot of the Pi2. Go ahead and click the **Yes** button. After reboot, the next step is to update and upgrade the Pi2 or Pi3 software. Go ahead and click on the **Terminal** icon located at the top left of the Pi2 or Pi3 monitor (see the following screenshot):

Terminal icon

After the **Terminal** window appears, enter sudo apt-get update at the $ prompt (see the following screenshot):

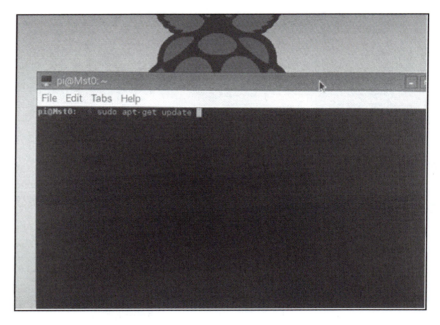

Terminal screen

This update process takes several minutes. After the update concludes, enter sudo apt-get upgrade; again, this upgrade process takes several minutes. At the completion of the upgrade, enter at the $ prompt each of the following commands:

- sudo apt-get install build-essential
- sudo apt-get install manpages-dev
- sudo apt-get install gfortran
- sudo apt-get install nfs-common
- sudo apt-get install nfs-kernel-server
- sudo apt-get install vim
- sudo apt-get install openmpi-bin
- sudo apt-get install libopenmpi-dev
- sudo apt-get install openmpi-doc
- sudo apt-get install keychain
- sudo apt-get install nmap

These updates and installs will allow you to edit (`vim`) and run Fortran, C, MPI codes, and allow you to manipulate and further configure your master Pi2 or Pi3. We will now transfer codes from the main PC to the master Pi2 or Pi3.

Transferring the code

The next step is to transfer your codes from the main PC to the master Pi2 or Pi3, after which you will again compile and run the codes, much like you did earlier. But before we proceed, you need to ascertain the IP address of the master Pi2 or Pi3. Go ahead and enter the `ifconfig` command, in the Pi terminal window (see the following screenshot):

IP address

The author's Pi2 IP address is `192.168.0.9` (see the second line of the displayed text). The MAC address is `b8:27:eb:81:e5:7d` (see the first line of the displayed text), and the net mask address is `255.255.255.0`. Write down these numbers, as they will be needed later when configuring the Pis and switch.

Your IP address may be similar, possibly except for the last two highlighted numbers depicted earlier. Return to your main PC, and list the contents in the code folder located in the `Desktop` directory; that is, type and enter `ls -la`. The list of the folder content is displayed. You can now **Secure File Transfer Protocol (SFTP)** your codes to your master Pi. Note the example in the following screenshot. The author's processor name is `gamma` in the Ubuntu/Linux environment:

```
carlospg@gamma:~$ cd Desktop/PI_Paper/Master_Pi2/Book_b
carlospg@gamma:~/Desktop/PI_Paper/Master_Pi2/Book_b$ ls -la
total 292
drwxrwxr-x 2 carlospg carlospg  4096 Sep 18 19:21 .
drwxrwxr-x 5 carlospg carlospg  4096 Sep 18 19:20 ..
-rwxrwxr-x 1 carlospg carlospg  8944 Sep 18 11:42 call-procs
-rw-rw-r-- 1 carlospg carlospg 10869 Sep 18 18:38 call-procs_a.odt
-rw-rw-r-- 1 carlospg carlospg   747 Sep 17 18:35 call-procs.c
-rw-rw-r-- 1 carlospg carlospg 10953 Sep 18 09:36 call-procs_c.odt
-rw-rw-r-- 1 carlospg carlospg 10958 Sep 18 11:53 call-procs_d.odt
-rw-rw-r-- 1 carlospg carlospg 15909 Sep 18 13:34 call-procs_e.odt
-rw-rw-r-- 1 carlospg carlospg 13163 Sep 18 11:38 call-procs.odt
-rwxrwxr-x 1 carlospg carlospg  8656 Sep 18 18:01 C_PI
-rw-rw-r-- 1 carlospg carlospg   660 Sep 18 18:10 C_PI.c
-rw-rw-r-- 1 carlospg carlospg 12825 Sep 18 12:29 C_PI.odt
-rw-rw-r-- 1 carlospg carlospg 10598 Sep 17 20:52 hosts3.odt
-rwxrwxr-x 1 carlospg carlospg 13400 Sep 12 16:23 MPI_06
-rw-rw-r-- 1 carlospg carlospg  1751 Sep 12 17:12 MPI_06.c
-rwxrwxr-x 1 carlospg carlospg 13400 Sep 17 17:40 MPI_07
-rw-rw-r-- 1 carlospg carlospg  1938 Sep 17 17:39 MPI_07.c
-rwxrwxr-x 1 carlospg carlospg 13400 Sep 17 19:30 MPI_08
-rwxrwxr-x 1 carlospg carlospg 13408 Sep 18 10:52 MPI_08_b
-rw-rw-r-- 1 carlospg carlospg  2464 Sep 18 10:49 MPI_08_b.c
-rw-rw-r-- 1 carlospg carlospg 19789 Sep 18 11:09 MPI_08_b.odt
-rw-rw-r-- 1 carlospg carlospg  2406 Sep 17 19:33 MPI_08.c
-rw-rw-r-- 1 carlospg carlospg 13266 Sep 18 18:57 Pi_run_a.odt
-rw-rw-r-- 1 carlospg carlospg 13445 Sep 18 19:01 Pi_run_b.odt
-rw-rw-r-- 1 carlospg carlospg 10272 Sep 18 19:11 Pi_run_c.odt
-rw-rw-r-- 1 carlospg carlospg 12022 Sep 18 14:11 Pi_run.odt
carlospg@gamma:~/Desktop/PI_Paper/Master_Pi2/Book_b$ sftp pi@192.168.0.9
pi@192.168.0.9's password:
Connected to 192.168.0.9.
sftp> put MPI_08_b.c
Uploading MPI_08_b.c to /home/pi/MPI_08_b.c
MPI_08_b.c                       100% 2464   2.4KB/s   00:00
sftp> exit
carlospg@gamma:~/Desktop/PI_Paper/Master_Pi2/Book_b$
```

If you are not in the correct code folder, change the directory by typing `cd Desktop`, followed by the path to your code files. The author's files are stored in the `Book_b` folder. The requisite files are highlighted in red (see the preceding screenshot). At the `$` prompt, enter `sftp pi@192.168.0.9`, using, of course, your own Pi IP address following the `@` character.

You will be prompted for a password. Enter the password for your Pi. At the
`sftp>` prompt, enter `put MPI_08_b.c.`, again replacing the author's filename with your
own, if so desired. Go ahead and `sftp` the other files also. Next, enter `exit`. You should
now be back at your `code` folder (see the preceding screenshot).

Now, here comes the fun part. You will, from here onward, communicate remotely with
your Pi from your main PC, much like the way hackers do to remote computers. So go
ahead now and log into your master Pi. Enter `ssh pi@192.168.09` at the `$` prompt, and
enter your password. Now do a listing of the files in the home directory; enter `ls -la` (see
the following screenshot):

```
carlospg@gamma:~$ cd Desktop/PI_Paper/Master_Pi2/Book_b
carlospg@gamma:~/Desktop/PI_Paper/Master_Pi2/Book_b$ ssh pi@192.168.0.9
pi@192.168.0.9's password:

The programs included with the Debian GNU/Linux system are free software;
the exact distribution terms for each program are described in the
individual files in /usr/share/doc/*/copyright.

Debian GNU/Linux comes with ABSOLUTELY NO WARRANTY, to the extent
permitted by applicable law.
Last login: Wed Sep 21 08:52:42 2016
pi@Mst0:~ $ ls -la
total 272
drwxr-xr-x 18 pi  pi  4096 Sep 21 12:57 .
drwxr-xr-x  4 root root 4096 Sep  5 00:46 ..
-rw-r--r--  1 pi  pi    69 Sep  4 22:20 .asoundrc
-rw-------  1 pi  pi 10040 Sep 21 12:55 .bash_history
-rw-r--r--  1 pi  pi   220 May 27 07:09 .bash_logout
-rw-r--r--  1 pi  pi  3512 May 27 07:09 .bashrc
drwxr-xr-x  6 pi  pi  4096 May 27 07:50 .cache
-rwxr-xr-x  1 pi  pi  8944 Sep 21 12:52 calc-pi
-rwxr-xr-x  1 pi  pi  8944 Sep  7 15:21 calc-pi1
-rw-------  1 pi  pi  2188 Sep  7 15:15 calc-pi1.c
-rwxr-xr-x  1 pi  pi  8944 Sep  8 19:04 calc-pi2
-rw-------  1 pi  pi  2188 Sep  9 17:13 calc-pi2.c
-rw-------  1 pi  pi  2251 Sep 12 22:37 calc-pi.c
-rwxr-xr-x  1 pi  pi  6956 Sep  4 23:19 call-procs
-rw-r--r--  1 pi  pi   747 Sep 18 11:46 call-procs.c
drwxr-xr-x  9 pi  pi  4096 Sep  4 22:22 .config
-rwxr-xr-x  1 pi  pi  6664 Sep 15 20:04 C_PI
-rw-r--r--  1 pi  pi   530 Sep 15 20:04 C_PI.c
drwx------  3 pi  pi  4096 May 27 07:50 .dbus
drwxr-xr-x  2 pi  pi  4096 May 27 07:40 Desktop
drwxr-xr-x  5 pi  pi  4096 Sep  4 22:09 Documents
drwxr-xr-x  2 pi  pi  4096 May 27 07:50 Downloads
drwxr-xr-x  2 pi  pi  4096 Sep  4 22:18 .gstreamer-0.10
drwxr-xr-x  3 pi  pi  4096 Sep  4 22:09 .local
-rw-r--r--  1 pi  pi  2254 Sep 11 13:28 MPI_03.c
-rwxr-xr-x  1 pi  pi  9128 Sep 11 15:25 MPI_04
-rw-r--r--  1 pi  pi  1643 Sep 11 15:17 MPI_04.c
-rwxr-xr-x  1 pi  pi  9128 Sep 15 16:28 MPI_06
-rw-r--r--  1 pi  pi  1751 Sep 12 17:14 MPI_06.c
-rwxr-xr-x  1 pi  pi  9128 Sep 17 19:58 MPI_08
-rwxr-xr-x  1 pi  pi  9128 Sep 18 14:00 MPI_08_b
-rw-r--r--  1 pi  pi  2464 Sep 21 12:57 MPI_08_b.c
-rw-r--r--  1 pi  pi  2406 Sep 17 19:34 MPI_08.c
drwxr-xr-x  2 pi  pi  4096 May 27 07:50 Music
-rw-r--r--  1 pi  pi    50 Sep 18 15:18 ntwk_rst.sh
drwxr-xr-x  2 pi  pi  4096 May 27 07:50 Pictures
```

```
-rw-r--r--  1 pi  pi     675 May 27 07:09 .profile
drwxr-xr-x  2 pi  pi    4096 May 27 07:50 Public
drwxr-xr-x  2 pi  pi    4096 Sep  4 22:09 python_games
-rw-r--r--  1 pi  pi     183 Sep 17 23:05 reboot.sh
-rw-r--r--  1 root root   239 Sep 17 23:05 shutdown.sh
drwx------  2 pi  pi    4096 Sep  5 00:15 .ssh
-rw-r--r--  1 pi  pi      77 Sep 17 23:06 ssh.sh
drwxr-xr-x  2 pi  pi    4096 May 27 07:50 Templates
drwxr-xr-x  3 pi  pi    4096 Sep  4 22:09 .themes
drwxr-xr-x  2 pi  pi    4096 May 27 07:50 Videos
-rw-------  1 pi  pi    3997 Sep 21 12:54 .viminfo
-rw-------  1 pi  pi     105 Sep 21 08:52 .Xauthority
-rw-------  1 pi  pi     353 Sep 21 08:52 .xsession-errors
-rw-------  1 pi  pi     353 Sep 21 01:22 .xsession-errors.old
pi@Mst0:~ $
```

You should see the files (like the files shown in the preceding screenshot) in your home directory that you recently `sftp` over from your main PC. You can now roam around freely inside your Pi, and see what secret data can be stolen-never mind, I'm getting a little carried away here.

Go ahead and compile the requisite files, `call-procs.c`, `C_PI.c` and `MPI_08_b.c`, by entering the `mpicc [file name.c] -o [file name] -lm` command in each case. The `-lm` extension is required when compiling C files containing the math header file `<math.h>`, such as those example C files in later chapters of this book. Execute the `call-procs` file, or the filename you created, using the `mpiexec -n 1 call-procs` command. After the first execution, use a different process number in each subsequent execution. Your run should approximate to the following ones depicted. Note that because of the multithreaded nature of the program, the number of processes execute in random order, and there is clearly no dependence on one another:

```
pi@Mst0:~ $ mpiexec -n 1 call-procs
Calling process 0 out of 1 on Mst0
pi@Mst0:~ $ mpiexec -n 2 call-procs
Calling process 0 out of 2 on Mst0
Calling process 1 out of 2 on Mst0
pi@Mst0:~ $ mpiexec -n 3 call-procs
Calling process 2 out of 3 on Mst0
Calling process 0 out of 3 on Mst0
Calling process 1 out of 3 on Mst0
pi@Mst0:~ $ mpiexec -n 4 call-procs
Calling process 0 out of 4 on Mst0
Calling process 3 out of 4 on Mst0
Calling process 1 out of 4 on Mst0
Calling process 2 out of 4 on Mst0
pi@Mst0:~ $
```

From here onward, the run data was from a Pi2 computer. The Pi3 computer will give a faster runtime (its processor clock speed is 1.2 GHz, as compared to the Pi2, which has an overclocked speed of 1 GHz).

Execute the serial π code `C_PI`, as depicted in the following screenshot:

```
pi@Mst0:~ $ time mpiexec C_PI

Calculated Pi = 3.1415926535906125
       M_PI = 3.1415926535897931
Relative error = 0.0000000000008193

real    0m0.177s
user    0m0.080s
sys     0m0.080s
pi@Mst0:~ $
```

Execute the MPI π code `MPI_08_b`, as depicted in the following screenshot:

```
pi@Mst0:~ $ time mpiexec -n 4 MPI_08_b

############################################################

Master node name: Mst0

Enter the number of intervals:

300000


*** Number of processes: 4


    Calculated pi = 3.1415926535907128
         M_PI = 3.1415926535897931
    Relative Error = 0.0000000000009197

real    16m35.140s
user    63m3.610s
sys     0m2.630s
pi@Mst0:~ $
```

The difference in execution time between the four cores on gamma (0m59.076s), and the four cores on Mst0, is that each core in gamma is running at 4 GHz, while each core in Mst0 is running at 1 GHz. Core clock speed matters.

Preparing the slave node

You will now prepare/configure the first slave node of your supercomputer. Switch the HDMI monitor cable from the master Pi to the slave Pi. Check to see whether the SD NOOBS/Raspbian card is inserted in the drive. Label side should face outward. The drive is spring-loaded, so you must gently insert the card. To remove the card, apply a gentle inward pressure to unlock the card. Insert the slave power cord into a USB power slot adjacent the master Pi, in the rapid charger. Follow the same procedure outlined previously for installing, updating, and upgrading the Raspbian OS on the master Pi, this time naming the slave node Slv1, or any other name you desire.

Note that the author suggests that you use the same password for all the Pi2s or Pi3s in the cluster, as it simplifies the configuration procedure.

At the completion of the update, upgrade, and installation, acquire the IP address of the slave1 Pi, as you will be remotely logging into it. Use the ifconfig command to obtain its IP address. Return to your main PC, and use sftp to transfer the requisite files from your main computer – much like you did for the master Pi2. Compile the transferred .c files. Test/run the codes as discussed earlier. You are now ready to configure the master Pi and slave Pi for communication between themselves and the main PC.

Summary

In this chapter, a list of parts for your Pi2 or Pi3 supercomputer was presented. We then proceeded to learn about the genesis of the Pi microcomputer, and its all-important technical specs. Next, we configured the master node, and subsequently transferred the requisite codes from the main PC to the master node. Finally, the slave1 node was configured to create an initial two-node Pi supercomputer. In Chapter 4, *Static IP Address and Hosts File Setup*, we will learn how to set up the static IP address and hosts file on the master and slave1 nodes.

4
Static IP Address and Hosts File Setup

Some network switches don't allow the connected computers to set their own static IP address if they are using a dynamic configuration, so in that case we should reconfigure the switch and set up the static IP addresses of the nodes in the switch ourselves. Stable operation of the supercomputer requires that the IP address in the Pi nodes and on the switch remain unchanged during normal operation. Otherwise, the nodes will be unable to communicate with each other, thus making the supercomputer's performance less than optimal. This configuration procedure is accompanied by the setup of the hosts file.

In this chapter, you will learn how to do the following:

- Configure the static IP address of the master and slave1 Pi
- Configure the static IP address of the network switch
- Set up the hosts file

Configuring static IP address of the master Pi

Note the IP address for the master (Mst0) and slave (Slv1) Pi by using the `ifconfig` command discussed in Chapter 3, *Preparing the Initial Two Nodes*. Go ahead and `ssh` into the master node from the main PC, and edit the network `interfaces` file. Enter `sudo vim /etc/network/interfaces`. The editor opens the file, displaying the following contents:

```
# interfaces(5) file used by ifup(8) and ifdown(8)

# Please note that this file is written to be used with dhcpcd
# For static IP, consult /etc/dhcpcd.conf and 'man dhcpcd.conf'

# Include files from /etc/network/interfaces.d:
source-directory /etc/network/interfaces.d

auto lo
iface lo inet loopback

# iface eth0 inet manual
iface eth0 inet static
address 192.168.0.9
netmask 255.255.255.0

allow-hotplug wlan0
iface wlan0 inet manual
    wpa-conf /etc/wpa_supplicant/wpa_supplicant.conf

allow-hotplug wlan1
iface wlan1 inet manual
    wpa-conf /etc/wpa_supplicant/wpa_supplicant.conf
```

Insert the text highlighted in red; note the IP address and netmask address. These were ascertained earlier. The text `iface etho inet manuel` is commented out with #, and replaced with `iface eth0 inet static`; underneath that is the master Pi IP address, and next to that is the netmask address. Save the changes by entering `Esc:wq`, that is, colon `wq`, (colon (:), write (`w`), and quit (`q`)). You should now be back at the `pi@Mst0:~ $` prompt. You now want to restart the network interface by entering, at the `$` prompt, the `sudo /etc/init.d/networking restart` command. Repeat the same procedure for the slave (Slv1) node, updating appropriately its IP address in the interfaces file. The following narrative walks you through the process of setting the static IP addresses in the switch.

Configuring a network switch static IP address

Some network switches don't allow the connected computers to set their own static IP address if they are using a dynamic configuration, so in that case we should proceed to the switch's configuration and set up the static IP addresses ourselves. The following procedure relates to the HP 1910-8 managed switch from your parts list. First, remove your router's Ethernet cable from the switch (see the following figure); otherwise, you will be prompted (during attempted login to the switch) for your router's login information:

Router Ethernet cable

Next, connect the other end of the switch's Ethernet cable to the main PC USB port (see the following figure). This special cable is supplied with the switch:

Switch Ethernet cable

The following figure shows the extra Ethernet patch cable extending from the main PC Ethernet port, and connecting to the switch's Ethernet port used for communicating with the Pis:

Main PC Ethernet cable

Unplug the switch's power cord for a couple of seconds, and then reinsert the plug. This action causes the switch to reboot. The reboot will last approximately 2 minutes, as the switch learns/generates the MAC addresses of the two Pis, and allows access to the switch's configuration window. Once the switch comes back online (as indicated by the green blinking LED lights on the front panel), go back to your main computer, and open a web browser (in the Windows environment) of your preference. Enter the switch's IP address in the browser (consult the user's manual for the login IP address for your device; the author's switch's IP address was 169.254.76.230). Upon entering the IP address, a login window appears. Enter admin for the username, and then type the password shown on the right side of the input field.

 The password changes each time you log in to the switch.

You now have access to the switch's configuration window depicted in the following screenshot. Click on the **Network** tab. You are now presented with a drop-down menu. Click on the **MAC** tab. This opens a window similar in appearance to the screenshot. The screenshot shows the **MAC** address settings of the author's eight Pis in his Pi2 super cluster. Initially, the addresses were learned, and designated dynamic. You should convert these addresses to the static setting.

You achieve this by clicking on the **Add** button and then filling in the appropriate fields to make each address static. At this point, however, you will see only two MAC addresses, as you have not yet powered up the remaining six Pi2s or Pi3s for their MAC address to be learned:

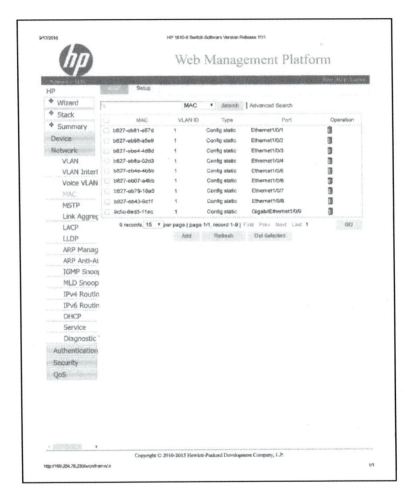

The next step is to type in the static IP address associated with the static **MAC** address. Move down the menu to **ARP Managed,** select this tab. A window appears allowing you access to the IP settings.

Again, click on the **Add** button, and fill in the appropriate fields for making the address static. **Save** these settings by clicking on the **Save** link at the top-right-hand side of the web page. Wait a few moments while the information is being saved, then click on the **Logout** link. If you encounter difficulties, contact HP customer service. They will be more than happy to assist you:

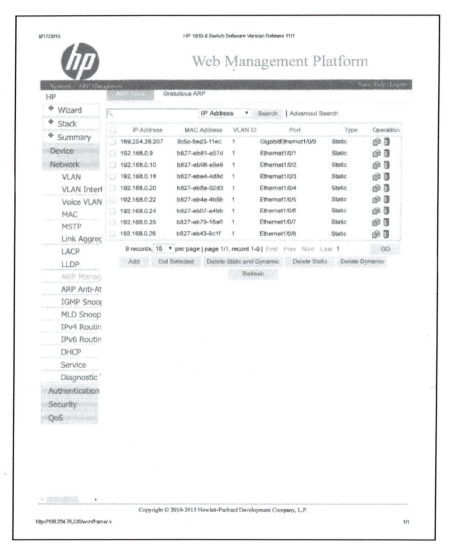

Close the browser and unplug the switch's power cord. Re-insert the router's Ethernet cable into the switch, and disconnect the switch's Ethernet cable from the main PC. Re-insert the switch's power cord. This will reboot the switch, which takes a few minutes. We are now poised for some intense geeking. Okay, so return now to your main PC, and check that your Pis are still alive. Open the terminal window in the Linux environment, and enter `ping 192.168.0.9` (or your equivalent master IP address) to see whether the master Pi responds. If it is still alive, you should see a series of statements, as shown in the following screenshot. Terminate the ping run by entering *Ctrl+C*. Do this also for the slave Pi:

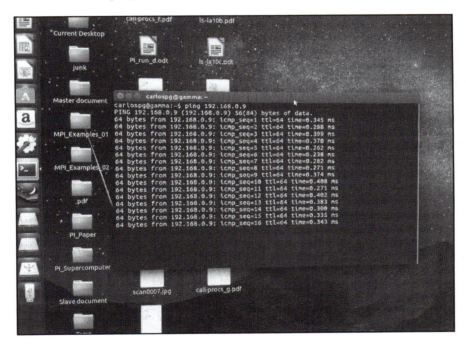

Ping responses displayed in terminal window

Once you have determined that the Pis are alive, `ssh pi@192.168.0.9` into the master Pi node. Once you are in the master node, `ssh` into the slave Pi node using the command you used before, that is, `ssh pi@192.168.0.10`; however, because we are using the master node, and because we are using the `pi` user, it is not necessary to use `pi@` before the IP address. So instead type `ssh 192.168.0.9` and it will log you in from the master node to the slave node (see command statements highlighted in red in the following screenshot):

```
carlospg@gamma:~$ ssh pi@192.168.0.9
pi@192.168.0.9's password:

The programs included with the Debian GNU/Linux system are free software;
the exact distribution terms for each program are described in the
individual files in /usr/share/doc/*/copyright.

Debian GNU/Linux comes with ABSOLUTELY NO WARRANTY, to the extent
permitted by applicable law.
Last login: Sun Sep 25 10:12:28 2016 from 192.168.0.11
pi@Mst0:~ $ ssh 192.168.0.10
pi@192.168.0.10's password:

The programs included with the Debian GNU/Linux system are free software;
the exact distribution terms for each program are described in the
individual files in /usr/share/doc/*/copyright.

Debian GNU/Linux comes with ABSOLUTELY NO WARRANTY, to the extent
permitted by applicable law.
Last login: Sun Sep 25 10:16:22 2016 from mst0
pi@Slv1:~ $
```

Go ahead and list the files on the slave node (see the following screenshot):

```
pi@Slv1:~ $ ls -la
total 140
drwxr-xr-x 18 pi  pi  4096 Sep 25 01:29 .
drwxr-xr-x  4 root root 4096 Sep  5 09:01 ..
-rw-r--r--  1 pi  pi    69 Sep  4 19:52 .asoundrc
-rw-------  1 pi  pi  2817 Sep 22 23:50 .bash_history
-rw-r--r--  1 pi  pi   220 May 27 07:09 .bash_logout
-rw-r--r--  1 pi  pi  3512 May 27 07:09 .bashrc
drwxr-xr-x  6 pi  pi  4096 May 27 07:50 .cache
-rwxr-xr-x  1 pi  pi  8944 Sep  4 20:55 calc-pi
-rw-------  1 pi  pi  2188 Sep  4 20:54 calc-pi.c
-rwxr-xr-x  1 pi  pi  6956 Sep  4 20:56 call-procs
-rw-r--r--  1 pi  pi   814 Sep  4 20:54 call-procs.c
drwxr-xr-x  9 pi  pi  4096 Sep  4 19:53 .config
drwx------  3 pi  pi  4096 May 27 07:50 .dbus
drwxr-xr-x  2 pi  pi  4096 May 27 07:40 Desktop
drwxr-xr-x  5 pi  pi  4096 Sep  4 19:01 Documents
drwxr-xr-x  2 pi  pi  4096 May 27 07:50 Downloads
drwxr-xr-x  2 pi  pi  4096 Sep  4 19:50 .gstreamer-0.10
drwxr-xr-x  3 pi  pi  4096 Sep  4 19:01 .local
drwxr-xr-x  2 pi  pi  4096 May 27 07:50 Music
-rw-r--r--  1 pi  pi    50 Sep 18 14:59 ntwk_rst.sh
drwxr-xr-x  2 pi  pi  4096 May 27 07:50 Pictures
-rw-r--r--  1 pi  pi   675 May 27 07:09 .profile
drwxr-xr-x  2 pi  pi  4096 May 27 07:50 Public
drwxr-xr-x  2 pi  pi  4096 Sep  4 19:01 python_games
drwx------  2 pi  pi  4096 Sep  5 00:13 .ssh
drwxr-xr-x  2 pi  pi  4096 May 27 07:50 Templates
drwxr-xr-x  3 pi  pi  4096 Sep  4 19:01 .themes
drwxr-xr-x  2 pi  pi  4096 May 27 07:50 Videos
-rw-------  1 pi  pi   829 Sep 18 15:02 .viminfo
-rw-------  1 pi  pi   105 Sep 25 01:29 .Xauthority
-rw-------  1 pi  pi   353 Sep 25 01:29 .xsession-errors
-rw-------  1 pi  pi   353 Sep 24 01:25 .xsession-errors.old
```

Now `ssh` back into the master node:

```
pi@Slv1:~ $ ssh 192.168.0.9
pi@192.168.0.9's password:

The programs included with the Debian GNU/Linux system are free software;
the exact distribution terms for each program are described in the
individual files in /usr/share/doc/*/copyright.

Debian GNU/Linux comes with ABSOLUTELY NO WARRANTY, to the extent
permitted by applicable law.
Last login: Sun Sep 25 10:17:19 2016 from 192.168.0.11
pi@Mst0:~ $
```

Go ahead and list the files on the master node (see the following screenshot):

```
pi@Mst0:~ $ ls -la
total 284
drwxr-xr-x 18 pi   pi    4096 Sep 25 01:29 .
drwxr-xr-x  4 root root  4096 Sep  5 00:46 ..
-rw-r--r--  1 pi   pi      69 Sep  4 22:20 .asoundrc
-rw-------  1 pi   pi   11211 Sep 25 10:16 .bash_history
-rw-r--r--  1 pi   pi     220 May 27 07:09 .bash_logout
-rw-r--r--  1 pi   pi    3512 May 27 07:09 .bashrc
drwxr-xr-x  6 pi   pi    4096 May 27 07:50 .cache
-rwxr-xr-x  1 pi   pi    8944 Sep 21 12:52 calc-pi
-rwxr-xr-x  1 pi   pi    8944 Sep  7 15:21 calc-pi1
-rw-------  1 pi   pi    2188 Sep  7 15:15 calc-pi1.c
-rwxr-xr-x  1 pi   pi    8944 Sep  8 19:04 calc-pi2
-rw-------  1 pi   pi    2188 Sep  9 17:13 calc-pi2.c
-rw-------  1 pi   pi    2251 Sep 12 22:37 calc-pi.c
-rwxr-xr-x  1 pi   pi    6956 Sep  4 23:19 call-procs
-rw-r--r--  1 pi   pi     747 Sep 18 11:46 call-procs.c
drwxr-xr-x  9 pi   pi    4096 Sep  4 22:22 .config
-rwxr-xr-x  1 pi   pi    6664 Sep 15 20:04 C_PI
-rw-r--r--  1 pi   pi     530 Sep 15 20:04 C_PI.c
drwx------  3 pi   pi    4096 May 27 07:50 .dbus
drwxr-xr-x  2 pi   pi    4096 May 27 07:40 Desktop
drwxr-xr-x  5 pi   pi    4096 Sep  4 22:09 Documents
drwxr-xr-x  2 pi   pi    4096 May 27 07:50 Downloads
drwxr-xr-x  2 pi   pi    4096 Sep  4 22:18 .gstreamer-0.10
drwxr-xr-x  3 pi   pi    4096 Sep  4 22:09 .local
-rw-r--r--  1 pi   pi    2254 Sep 11 13:28 MPI_03.c
-rwxr-xr-x  1 pi   pi    9128 Sep 11 15:25 MPI_04
-rw-r--r--  1 pi   pi    1643 Sep 11 15:17 MPI_04.c
-rwxr-xr-x  1 pi   pi    9128 Sep 15 16:28 MPI_06
-rw-r--r--  1 pi   pi    1751 Sep 12 17:14 MPI_06.c
-rwxr-xr-x  1 pi   pi    9128 Sep 17 19:58 MPI_08
-rwxr-xr-x  1 pi   pi    9128 Sep 18 14:00 MPI_08_b
-rw-r--r--  1 pi   pi    2464 Sep 21 12:57 MPI_08_b.c
-rw-r--r--  1 pi   pi    2406 Sep 17 19:34 MPI_08.c
drwxr-xr-x  2 pi   pi    4096 May 27 07:50 Music
-rw-r--r--  1 pi   pi      50 Sep 18 15:18 ntwk_rst.sh
drwxr-xr-x  2 pi   pi    4096 May 27 07:50 Pictures
-rw-r--r--  1 pi   pi     675 May 27 07:09 .profile
drwxr-xr-x  2 pi   pi    4096 May 27 07:50 Public
drwxr-xr-x  2 pi   pi    4096 Sep  4 22:09 python_games
-rw-r--r--  1 pi   pi     183 Sep 17 23:05 reboot.sh
-rw-r--r--  1 root root   239 Sep 17 23:05 shutdown.sh
drwx------  2 pi   pi    4096 Sep  5 00:15 .ssh
-rw-r--r--  1 pi   pi      77 Sep 17 23:06 ssh.sh
drwxr-xr-x  2 pi   pi    4096 May 27 07:50 Templates
drwxr-xr-x  3 pi   pi    4096 Sep  4 22:09 .themes
-rw-r--r--  1 pi   pi     233 Sep 22 13:12 update.sh
-rw-r--r--  1 pi   pi     240 Sep 22 13:13 upgrade.sh
```

```
drwxr-xr-x 2 pi  pi   4096 May 27 07:50 Videos
-rw------- 1 pi  pi   4297 Sep 22 13:13 .viminfo
-rw------- 1 pi  pi   105 Sep 25 01:29 .Xauthority
-rw------- 1 pi  pi   353 Sep 25 01:29 .xsession-errors
-rw------- 1 pi  pi   353 Sep 24 01:25 .xsession-errors.old
pi@Mst0:~ $
```

This is great, because you can now access one node from another node, and you will also be able to do this from any node in the cluster. This also means that you can log in to any of the nodes in the cluster and reboot, `sudo reboot`, or shut them down, `sudo shutdown -h` now, remotely, without having to plug in any of the nodes into the **Pi Monitor**. Now, having to `ssh` into IP addresses all the time can get rather tedious, so let's try something new; that is, let's give each node a short name, such as `Mst0` for master and `Slv1` for slave node1, which will now allow you to `ssh` into a name instead of an IP address. To accomplish this, you will need to modify the `hosts` file.

Hosts file setup

First, open the `hosts` file, to see what's in there. Use the command highlighted in red:

```
pi@Mst0:~ $ cat /etc/hosts
127.0.0.1       localhost
::1             localhost ip6-localhost ip6-loopback
ff02::1         ip6-allnodes
ff02::2         ip6-allrouters

127.0.1.1       Mst0
```

Let's edit this file. You need to define a host name for a given address so that when you `ssh` the name, the Pis will recognize what IP address you are referring to. So, let's modify the `hosts` file (see the following screenshot). Enter the command `sudo vim /etc/hosts` and update the records with the highlighted text (substituting your own IP address):

```
127.0.0.1      localhost
::1            localhost ip6-localhost ip6-loopback
ff02::1        ip6-allnodes
ff02::2        ip6-allrouters

# 127.0.1.1    Mst0

192.168.0.9    Mst0
192.168.0.10   Slv1
```

 Remember to comment out `127.0.1.1 Mst0` with the # character, and then save the updated files by pressing the *Esc* key and entering `:wq`.

Now let's give this new technique a whirl. Enter the command `ssh Slv1` and then enter the password. The prompt should change to `pi@Slv1:~ $`. This means that we are now in the slave node1. Let's edit the same file in the slave node, by entering `sudo vim /etc/hosts`, and update the records with the highlighted text shown in the following screenshot, then save the updated file by entering `Esc:wq`:

```
127.0.0.1      localhost
::1            localhost ip6-localhost ip6-loopback
ff02::1        ip6-allnodes
ff02::2        ip6-allrouters

#127.0.1.1     Slv1

192.168.0.9    Mst0
192.168.0.10   Slv1
```

Go ahead and `ssh Mst0`, and enter the password. This takes you back to the master node: `pi@Mst0:~ $`. You can also `sudo ping Mst0` from the slave node to see whether the master node is alive, and vice versa. The appropriate results from these actions confirm that the hosts names were set up correctly.

Summary

In this chapter, we learned how to configure the static IP address on the Pi microcomputer, and the static IP address in the switch. We also updated the `hosts` file so you can `ssh` into a name instead of an IP address. The `Chapter 5`, *Creating a Common User for All Nodes*, will delve into creating a common user for all nodes.

5
Creating a Common User for All Nodes

Operating your supercomputer should be an effortless and pleasurable experience as you wield its massive power to crunch through difficult problems. Therefore, to facilitate this ease of use, we must create a common user for all nodes. This common user ties all the nodes together in one fell swoop, allowing you and the nodes to seamlessly communicate among themselves.

In this chapter, you will learn how to do the following:

- Create a new user for the master node
- Create a password for the new user on the master node
- Create a new user for the slave1 node
- Create a password for the new user on the slave1 node
- Generate a special key on the master node for **ssh**ing effortlessly between the nodes in the supercomputer without using a password
- Copy the special key from the master node to the slave1 node
- Edit the .bashrc file on the master node to facilitate seamless special key access to all the nodes
- Use the which command

Adding a new user for all nodes

We now proceed to implement the task components outlined earlier. First, we will add a new user to the pi home directory that will have the same user ID for all pi nodes at once. So, go ahead and list the current content of the home directory: enter ls -la /home at the $ prompt; see the following screenshot:

```
pi@Mst0:~ $ ls -la /home
total 16
drwxr-xr-x  4 root root 4096 Sep 5 00:46 .
drwxr-xr-x 22 root root 4096 Sep 5 14:27 ..
drwxr-xr-x 18 pi   pi   4096 Sep 22 13:13 pi
pi@Mst0:~ $
```

You see that it contains only the pi user. Now enter sudo useradd -m -u 1960 alpha. The parameter -m specifies the home directory, -u is the argument for a new user ID, 1960 is your new user ID (or any integer you desire), and the name alpha (or any name you desire) is what you want to associate with the user ID 1960. Now check to see whether the alpha, or the username you chose, was added to the home directory. List the contents as you did earlier; see the following screenshot:

```
pi@Mst0:~ $ ls -la /home
total 16
drwxr-xr-x  4 root  root  4096 Sep 5 00:46 .
drwxr-xr-x 22 root  root  4096 Sep 5 14:27 ..
drwxr-xr-x  5 alpha alpha 4096 Sep 21 09:32 alpha
drwxr-xr-x 18 pi    pi    4096 Sep 22 13:13 pi
pi@Mst0:~ $
```

You see that the alpha user was indeed added to the pi home directory. This is great! The next thing you want to do is create a password for this newly created alpha user, so enter the command sudo passwd alpha, and enter a new password; see the following screenshot:

```
pi@Mst0:~ $ sudo passwd alpha
Enter new UNIX password:
Retype new UNIX password:
passwd: password updated successfully
```

For convenience, the author used the same password as that used for the Pi nodes.

Go ahead now and log in as the newly minted `alpha` user. Enter `su - alpha` (note there is a space before and after the hyphen). Enter your password, and you are now logged in as the `alpha` user (see the following screenshot). Enter `exit`; you will be returned to the previous `pi` user:

```
pi@Mst0:~ $ su - alpha
Password:
alpha@Mst0:~ $ exit
logout
pi@Mst0:~ $
```

Now `ssh` into the slave node (`Slv1`) and repeat the steps you just completed. Enter `ssh Slv1`, and enter your password (the author used the same password for all his nodes for convenience).

ID key generation

You now have the `alpha` user on the slave1 node that will be running all the MPI programs. Let's now generate a special key that will allow you to `ssh` from one node to the next, or from the master node to all the slaves in the cluster, without having to insert the password multiple times. First, enter the command `ssh Mst0`, and enter the password, or enter `exit` to return to the master node, and then log in again as the `alpha` user; that is, enter the command `su - alpha`. At the $ prompt, enter `ssh-keygen -t rsa`. The `-t` is the argument, and `rsa` is a type of encryption. The first thing it's going to ask you for is a filename in which to save the key. Just save it in a default location by pressing the *Enter* key.

The next step is to enter a `passphrase`. Type in a `passphrase`. The author chose `atomic`; however, you can use any other name, if you so desire (note the characters are invisible), and re-enter the `passphrase`. You should see an image of the encrypted key like the one depicted in the following screenshot:

```
alpha@Mst0:~ $ ssh-keygen -t rsa
Generating public/private rsa key pair.
Enter file in which to save the key (/home/alpha/.ssh/id_rsa):
Created directory '/home/alpha/.ssh'.
Enter passphrase (empty for no passphrase):
Enter same passphrase again:
Your identification has been saved in /home/alpha/.ssh/id_rsa.
Your public key has been saved in /home/alpha/.ssh/id_rsa.pub.
The key fingerprint is:
1b:d8:a9:f6:b0:60:2c:8e:f1:dc:6a:54:20:d9:af:3d alpha@Mst0
The key's randomart image is:
+---[RSA 2048]----+
|  o              |
|o o              |
|. o              |
|  o o.           |
|  + .S           |
| o.E .o          |
|... +.+ .        |
|*.+ o +          |
|..=.. . .        |
+-----------------+
```

The next thing you should do is to copy this key over to the slave1 node.

ID key transfer

Enter the command `ssh-copy-id alpha@Slv1`; `alpha` is the username that will receive the key, and `Slv1` is the host which it belongs to. Enter the password for `Slv1` (see the highlighted commands in the following screenshot):

```
alpha@Mst0:~ $ ssh-copy-id alpha@Slv1
The authenticity of host 'slv1 (192.168.0.10)' can't be established.
ECDSA key fingerprint is c5:00:f7:64:ad:8d:65:22:9d:35:a9:42:0c:55:3d:43.
Are you sure you want to continue connecting (yes/no)? yes
/usr/bin/ssh-copy-id: INFO: attempting to log in with the new key(s), to filter out any that are already
installed
/usr/bin/ssh-copy-id: INFO: 1 key(s) remain to be installed -- if you are prompted now it is to install the
new keys
alpha@slv1's password:
Permission denied, please try again.
alpha@slv1's password:

Number of key(s) added: 1

Now try logging into the machine, with:   "ssh 'alpha@Slv1'"
and check to make sure that only the key(s) you wanted were added.
```

Oops! Entered the incorrect password. That's it! You have transferred the key. Now `ssh` into `Slv1`. It's now asking for a `passphrase` instead of a password; see the following screenshot. Enter the `passphrase` you provided earlier. This is great!

```
alpha@Mst0:~ $ ssh Slv1
Enter passphrase for key '/home/alpha/.ssh/id_rsa':

The programs included with the Debian GNU/Linux system are free software;
the exact distribution terms for each program are described in the
individual files in /usr/share/doc/*/copyright.

Debian GNU/Linux comes with ABSOLUTELY NO WARRANTY, to the extent
permitted by applicable law.
alpha@Slv1:~ $
```

Now `ssh` back into `Mst0`, and list the files in the `alpha` user by entering `ls -la`. We can see the `.ssh` folder. Go ahead and list the files in the `.ssh` folder (see the following screenshot):

```
alpha@Mst0:~ $ ls -la
total 28
drwxr-xr-x 3 alpha alpha 4096 Sep  5 09:38 .
drwxr-xr-x 4 root  root  4096 Sep  5 00:46 ..
-rw------- 1 alpha alpha    5 Sep  5 01:02 .bash_history
-rw-r--r-- 1 alpha alpha  220 Oct 18 2014 .bash_logout
-rw-r--r-- 1 alpha alpha 3512 May 27 07:09 .bashrc
-rw-r--r-- 1 alpha alpha  675 Oct 18 2014 .profile
drwx------ 2 alpha alpha 4096 Sep  5 09:52 .ssh
alpha@Mst0:~ $ ls -la .ssh
total 20
drwx------ 2 alpha alpha 4096 Sep  5 09:52 .
drwxr-xr-x 3 alpha alpha 4096 Sep  5 09:38 ..
-rw------- 1 alpha alpha 1766 Sep  5 09:40 id_rsa
-rw-r--r-- 1 alpha alpha  392 Sep  5 09:40 id_rsa.pub
-rw-r--r-- 1 alpha alpha  444 Sep  5 09:52 known_hosts
```

We now see the authorized keys `id_rsa`, `id_rsa.pub`, `known_hosts`. Now `ssh` into the `Slv1` node:

```
alpha@Mst0:~ $ ssh Slv1
Enter passphrase for key '/home/alpha/.ssh/id_rsa':

The programs included with the Debian GNU/Linux system are free software;
the exact distribution terms for each program are described in the
individual files in /usr/share/doc/*/copyright.

Debian GNU/Linux comes with ABSOLUTELY NO WARRANTY, to the extent
permitted by applicable law.
Last login: Mon Sep  5 10:33:36 2016 from mst0
```

We see that it is asking for a `passphrase`. This is not what we are looking for, so we still must make a few changes to our master node. Enter the `passphrase`, and enter `exit`. You should now have returned to the master node, `pi@Mst0:~ $`. If you are not now at the master node, close out the terminal window, and `ssh` back into the master node, and proceed; in other words, enter `ssh pi@192.168.0.9` and provide the password. Log into the `alpha` user by entering, at the $ prompt, `su - alpha`. You should now be at the `alpha` user prompt, `alpha@Mst0:~ $`. We are now going to edit a file called `.bashrc` within our `home` directory. Enter `vim .bashrc`, and then `i` to initiate editing. This opens a large file shown on the next few pages. Go to the bottom of the file and add the highlighted text, and then save the updated file by pressing the *Esc* key and entering `:wq`:

```
# ~/.bashrc: executed by bash(1) for non-login shells.
# see /usr/share/doc/bash/examples/startup-files (in the package bash-doc)
# for examples

# If not running interactively, don't do anything
case $- in
  *i*) ;;
    *) return;;
esac

# don't put duplicate lines or lines starting with space in the history.
# See bash(1) for more options
HISTCONTROL=ignoreboth

# append to the history file, don't overwrite it
shopt -s histappend

# for setting history length see HISTSIZE and HISTFILESIZE in bash(1)
HISTSIZE=1000
HISTFILESIZE=2000

# check the window size after each command and, if necessary,
# update the values of LINES and COLUMNS.
shopt -s checkwinsize

# If set, the pattern "**" used in a pathname expansion context will
# match all files and zero or more directories and subdirectories.
#shopt -s globstar

# make less more friendly for non-text input files, see lesspipe(1)
#[ -x /usr/bin/lesspipe ] && eval "$(SHELL=/bin/sh lesspipe)"

# set variable identifying the chroot you work in (used in the prompt below)
if [ -z "${debian_chroot:-}" ] && [ -r /etc/debian_chroot ]; then
    debian_chroot=$(cat /etc/debian_chroot)
fi

# set a fancy prompt (non-color, unless we know we "want" color)
case "$TERM" in
    xterm-color) color_prompt=yes;;
esac

# uncomment for a colored prompt, if the terminal has the capability; turned
# off by default to not distract the user: the focus in a terminal window
# should be on the output of commands, not on the prompt
force_color_prompt=yes

if [ -n "$force_color_prompt" ]; then
    if [ -x /usr/bin/tput ] && tput setaf 1 >&/dev/null; then
```

```
      # We have color support; assume it's compliant with Ecma-48
      # (ISO/IEC-6429). (Lack of such support is extremely rare, and such
      # a case would tend to support setf rather than setaf.)
      color_prompt=yes
    else
      color_prompt=
    fi
  fi

  if [ "$color_prompt" = yes ]; then
    PS1='${debian_chroot:+($debian_chroot)}\[\033[01;32m\]\u@\h\[\033[00m\]:\[\033[01;34m\]\w \$\
[\033[00m\] '
  else
    PS1='${debian_chroot:+($debian_chroot)}\u@\h:\w\$ '
  fi
  unset color_prompt force_color_prompt

  # If this is an xterm set the title to user@host:dir
  case "$TERM" in
  xterm*|rxvt*)
    PS1="\[\e]0;${debian_chroot:+($debian_chroot)}\u@\h: \w\a\]$PS1"
    ;;
  *)
    ;;
  esac

  # enable color support of ls and also add handy aliases
  if [ -x /usr/bin/dircolors ]; then
    test -r ~/.dircolors && eval "$(dircolors -b ~/.dircolors)" || eval "$(dircolors -b)"
    alias ls='ls --color=auto'
    #alias dir='dir --color=auto'
    #alias vdir='vdir --color=auto'

    alias grep='grep --color=auto'
    alias fgrep='fgrep --color=auto'
    alias egrep='egrep --color=auto'
  fi

  # colored GCC warnings and errors
  #export GCC_COLORS='error=01;31:warning=01;35:note=01;36:caret=01;32:locus=01:quote=01'

  # some more ls aliases
  #alias ll='ls -l'
  #alias la='ls -A'
  #alias l='ls -CF'

  # Alias definitions.
  # You may want to put all your additions into a separate file like
  # ~/.bash_aliases, instead of adding them here directly.
```

```
  # See /usr/share/doc/bash-doc/examples in the bash-doc package.

  if [ -f ~/.bash_aliases ]; then
    . ~/.bash_aliases
  fi

  # enable programmable completion features (you don't need to enable
  # this, if it's already enabled in /etc/bash.bashrc and /etc/profile
  # sources /etc/bash.bashrc).
  if ! shopt -oq posix; then
    if [ -f /usr/share/bash-completion/bash_completion ]; then
      . /usr/share/bash-completion/bash_completion
    elif [ -f /etc/bash_completion ]; then
      . /etc/bash_completion
    fi
  fi

  # Logic for keychain
  /usr/bin/keychain $HOME/.ssh/id_rsa
  source $HOME/.keychain/$HOSTNAME-sh
```

The highlighted text is where the `keychain` logic that you are going to be using resides. The `keychain` component calls the `keychain` command located in the `keychain` file. The `.ssh` component passes in the parameter/path of the location of the ID file `id_rsa`. The `source $HOME/.keychain/$HOSTNAME-sh` command runs the `$HOSTNAME-sh` file. You should now recompile the `.bashrc` file. So enter `source .bashrc` and provide the `passphrase` one more time (see the following highlighted text):

```
alpha@Mst0:~ $ vim .bashrc
alpha@Mst0:~ $ source .bashrc

 * keychain 2.7.1 ~ http://www.funtoo.org
 * Starting ssh-agent...
 * Starting gpg-agent...
 * Adding 1 ssh key(s): /home/alpha/.ssh/id_rsa
Enter passphrase for /home/alpha/.ssh/id_rsa:
 * ssh-add: Identities added: /home/alpha/.ssh/id_rsa
```

You can enter `which keychain` to uncover the path to `keychain`.

Go ahead and enter `ssh Slv1`:

```
alpha@Mst0:~ $ ssh Slv1

The programs included with the Debian GNU/Linux system are free software;
the exact distribution terms for each program are described in the
individual files in /usr/share/doc/*/copyright.

Debian GNU/Linux comes with ABSOLUTELY NO WARRANTY, to the extent
permitted by applicable law.
Last login: Mon Sep  5 10:46:38 2016 from mst0
alpha@Slv1:~ $
```

This time you were not prompted for the `passphrase`. Excellent!

Summary

In this chapter, we learned how to create a common user for all nodes. We achieved this by initially creating a new user for the master node, and then creating a password for that new user. We then employed a similar procedure for the slave1 node. Next, we generated a special key on the master node, copied the special key to the slave1 node, and then edited the `.bashrc` file on the master node to facilitate seamless special key access to all nodes in the super cluster. Finally, we used the `which` command to uncover the path to `keychain`. `Chapter 6`, *Creating a Mountable Drive on the Master Node*, discuss how to create a mountable drive on the master node. Go ahead and exit to the `pi` user `pi@Mst0:~ $`. If you are not now at the master node, close out the terminal window, `ssh` back into the master node.

6
Creating a Mountable Drive on the Master Node

This chapter discusses how to create a mountable drive on the master node. Effective, error-free operation of the Pi supercomputer requires that the slave nodes have the ability to mount the master node `export` drive/folder that contains the MPI code, so that each node will have their own identical code for carrying out a given task. In addition, you will be introduced to the powerful `-H` command, which can be employed to willfully task any or all threads, nodes, and cores to solve a given problem.

In this chapter, you will learn:

- How to use the `mkdir` command to make an `export` drive (used as an MPI code repository) on the master node.
- How to use the `chown` command to change ownership of the `export` drive from the `root` user to a new user.
- How to use the `rpcbind` command, which will allow the master Pi to export the `export` drive on the master node to the slave nodes.
- How to edit the `exports` file that will facilitate exporting the `export` drive on the master node to the slave nodes.
- How to use the `nfs-kernel-server` command.
- How to edit the bootup script `rc.local` file. On bootup, this file makes the `export` drive on the master node mountable for use by the slave nodes.
- How to use the `mount` command to manually mount the `export` drive containing the MPI codes.

- How to use the `cat` command for displaying the contents of a file.
- How to use the `cp -a` command to copy files/codes to the `export` drive.
- How to use the `-H` command to task any or all nodes and cores to work on a given problem.

Go ahead now and list all the folders/files in the `root` directory (see the following screenshot):

```
pi@Mst0:~ $ ls -la /
total 92
drwxr-xr-x 21 root root  4096 May 27 07:50 .
drwxr-xr-x 21 root root  4096 May 27 07:50 ..
drwxr-xr-x  2 root root  4096 Sep  4 22:09 bin
drwxr-xr-x  3 root root 16384 Dec 31  1969 boot
drwxr-xr-x 14 root root  3440 Sep  5 08:50 dev
drwxr-xr-x 111 root root 4096 Sep  5 00:54 etc
drwxr-xr-x  4 root root  4096 Sep  5 00:46 home
drwxr-xr-x 19 root root  4096 Sep  4 22:09 lib
drwx------  2 root root 16384 May 27 07:43 lost+found
drwxr-xr-x  3 root root  4096 Sep  4 22:17 media
drwxr-xr-x  2 root root  4096 May 27 07:04 mnt
drwxr-xr-x  7 root root  4096 Sep  4 22:09 opt
dr-xr-xr-x 158 root root    0 Dec 31  1969 proc
drwx------  2 root root  4096 Sep  5 00:38 root
drwxr-xr-x 20 root root   700 Sep  5 01:08 run
drwxr-xr-x  2 root root  4096 Sep  4 22:56 sbin
drwxr-xr-x  2 root root  4096 May 27 07:04 srv
dr-xr-xr-x 12 root root    0 Dec 31  1969 sys
drwxrwxrwt 13 root root  4096 Sep  5 13:17 tmp
drwxr-xr-x 11 root root  4096 Sep  4 22:17 usr
drwxr-xr-x 11 root root  4096 May 27 07:50 var
```

Let's now make a new drive in the `root` directory. We will call it `beta`, or whatever name you prefer. Enter `sudo mkdir /beta`, and again list all the files in the `root` directory (see the following screenshot). Enter `ls -la /`. You see now that we have a brand new `beta` drive:

```
pi@Mst0:~ $ ls -la /
total 96
drwxr-xr-x  22 root root   4096 Sep  5 14:27 .
drwxr-xr-x  22 root root   4096 Sep  5 14:27 ..
drwxr-xr-x   2 root root   4096 Sep  5 14:27 beta
drwxr-xr-x   2 root root   4096 Sep  4 22:09 bin
drwxr-xr-x   3 root root  16384 Dec 31  1969 boot
drwxr-xr-x  14 root root   3440 Sep  5 08:50 dev
drwxr-xr-x 111 root root   4096 Sep  5 00:54 etc
drwxr-xr-x   4 root root   4096 Sep  5 00:46 home
drwxr-xr-x  19 root root   4096 Sep  4 22:09 lib
drwx------   2 root root  16384 May 27 07:43 lost+found
drwxr-xr-x   3 root root   4096 Sep  4 22:17 media
drwxr-xr-x   2 root root   4096 May 27 07:04 mnt
drwxr-xr-x   7 root root   4096 Sep  4 22:09 opt
dr-xr-xr-x 158 root root      0 Dec 31  1969 proc
drwx------   2 root root   4096 Sep  5 00:38 root
drwxr-xr-x  20 root root    700 Sep  5 01:08 run
drwxr-xr-x   2 root root   4096 Sep  4 22:56 sbin
drwxr-xr-x   2 root root   4096 May 27 07:04 srv
dr-xr-xr-x  12 root root      0 Sep  5 14:15 sys
drwxrwxrwt  13 root root   4096 Sep  5 14:17 tmp
drwxr-xr-x  11 root root   4096 Sep  4 22:17 usr
drwxr-xr-x  11 root root   4096 May 27 07:50 var
```

You now want to change the owner, because we want it to belong to the `alpha` user. So go ahead and enter `sudo chown alpha:alpha /beta/`. We use `sudo` because the previous ownership was the `root` user. Go ahead and relist the files in the `root` directory (see the following screenshot):

```
pi@Mst0:~ $ ls -la /
total 96
drwxr-xr-x  22 root  root   4096 Sep  5 14:27 .
drwxr-xr-x  22 root  root   4096 Sep  5 14:27 ..
drwxr-xr-x   2 alpha alpha  4096 Sep  5 14:27 beta
drwxr-xr-x   2 root  root   4096 Sep  4 22:09 bin
drwxr-xr-x   3 root  root  16384 Dec 31  1969 boot
drwxr-xr-x  14 root  root   3440 Sep  5 08:50 dev
drwxr-xr-x 111 root  root   4096 Sep  5 00:54 etc
drwxr-xr-x   4 root  root   4096 Sep  5 00:46 home
drwxr-xr-x  19 root  root   4096 Sep  4 22:09 lib
drwx------   2 root  root  16384 May 27 07:43 lost+found
drwxr-xr-x   3 root  root   4096 Sep  4 22:17 media
drwxr-xr-x   2 root  root   4096 May 27 07:04 mnt
drwxr-xr-x   7 root  root   4096 Sep  4 22:09 opt
dr-xr-xr-x 158 root  root      0 Dec 31  1969 proc
drwx------   2 root  root   4096 Sep  5 00:38 root
drwxr-xr-x  20 root  root    700 Sep  5 01:08 run
drwxr-xr-x   2 root  root   4096 Sep  4 22:56 sbin
drwxr-xr-x   2 root  root   4096 May 27 07:04 srv
dr-xr-xr-x  12 root  root      0 Sep  5 14:15 sys
drwxrwxrwt  13 root  root   4096 Sep  5 14:17 tmp
drwxr-xr-x  11 root  root   4096 Sep  4 22:17 usr
drwxr-xr-x  11 root  root   4096 May 27 07:50 var
```

You see that beta is now set to the alpha user and alpha group. The next thing we want to do is to set up the rpcbind service. This will allow the master Pi to export the beta drive to the other slave nodes. So go ahead now and enter sudo rpcbind start. We also want to make sure that this service is always running every time you bootup the master Pi, so use the command; sudo update-rc.d rpcbind enable. This command will set a specific service to run whenever the Raspberry Pi boots up. Next, we need to specify which folder on the master node to make available for other nodes to mount, so you need to edit the exports file. Enter sudo vim /etc/exports. This opens the file for editing (see the following screenshot). Go ahead and add the text highlighted in red:

```
# /etc/exports: the access control list for filesystems which may be exported
#          to NFS clients.  See exports(5).
#
# Example for NFSv2 and NFSv3:
# /srv/homes       hostname1(rw,sync,no_subtree_check) hostname2(ro,sync,no_subtree_check)
#
# Example for NFSv4:
# /srv/nfs4        gss/krb5i(rw,sync,fsid=0,crossmnt,no_subtree_check)
# /srv/nfs4/homes  gss/krb5i(rw,sync,no_subtree_check)
#

# beta
/beta 192.168.0.0/24(rw,sync)
```

The first highlighted statement # beta, is a comment for the beta drive. The first argument /beta, is the folder on the master node that we want to export. The second argument 192.168.0.0/24 signifies that the IP addresses ranging from 192.168.0.0 to 192.168.0.255 will be allowed to mount the beta drive. rw means readable and writable. Enter Esc :wq to save the updated file.

You now need to restart the `nfs-kernel-server` service. So go ahead and enter the command; `sudo service nfs-kernel-server restart` (the author automated this command by inserting it at the bottom of the bootup script file `rc.local`. See highlighted text in the following screenshot). Enter `sudo vim /etc/rc.local` to edit this file, and then `Esc` `:wq`. Once this runs, the drive will be mountable:

```
#!/bin/sh -e
#
# rc.local
#
# This script is executed at the end of each multiuser runlevel.
# Make sure that the script will "exit 0" on success or any other
# value on error.
#
# In order to enable or disable this script just change the execution
# bits.
#
# By default this script does nothing.

# Print the IP address
_IP=$(hostname -I) || true
if [ "$_IP" ]; then
  printf "My IP address is %s\n" "$_IP"
fi

sudo service nfs-kernel-server restart

exit 0
```

Let's test this, switch to the slave `Slv1`, using the command; `ssh Slv1`. You should now be on the `slave` drive as indicated by the prompt `pi@Slv1:~ $`. Now enter the general command for mounting the `export` drive. Enter `sudo mount Mst0:/beta /beta` (see the following screenshot):

```
pi@Slv1:~ $ sudo mount Mst0:/beta /beta
mount.nfs: mount point /beta does not exist
pi@Slv1:~ $
```

Oops! We got an error message. The local mount point `beta` does not exist, so we must create this folder. Go ahead and list all the files in the `root` directories on the slave Pi (`Slv1`). See the following screenshot:

```
pi@Slv1:~ $ ls -la /
total 104
drwxr-xr-x 22 root root   4096 Sep  5 15:47 .
drwxr-xr-x 22 root root   4096 Sep  5 15:47 ..
drwxr-xr-x  2 root root   4096 Sep 22 11:05 bin
drwxr-xr-x  3 root root  16384 Dec 31  1969 boot
drwxr-xr-x 14 root root   3440 Sep 28 02:00 dev
drwxr-xr-x 111 root root  4096 Sep 25 21:35 etc
drwxr-xr-x  4 root root   4096 Sep  5 09:01 home
drwxr-xr-x 19 root root   4096 Sep 22 11:03 lib
drwx------  2 root root  16384 May 27 07:43 lost+found
drwxr-xr-x  3 root root   4096 Sep  4 19:50 media
drwxr-xr-x  2 root root   4096 May 27 07:04 mnt
drwxr-xr-x  7 root root   4096 Sep  4 18:59 opt
dr-xr-xr-x 147 root root     0 Dec 31  1969 proc
drwx------  2 root root   4096 Sep 25 21:35 root
drwxr-xr-x 20 root root    700 Sep 28 02:01 run
drwxr-xr-x  2 root root  12288 Sep 22 11:07 sbin
drwxr-xr-x  2 root root   4096 May 27 07:04 srv
dr-xr-xr-x 12 root root      0 Dec 31  1969 sys
drwxrwxrwt 11 root root   4096 Sep 28 16:00 tmp
drwxr-xr-x 11 root root   4096 Sep  4 19:49 usr
drwxr-xr-x 11 root root   4096 May 27 07:50 var
pi@Slv1:~ $
```

You will see that there is no `beta` folder. So go ahead and make a folder called `beta` in the `root` directory, similar to what you did on the master node. Enter the command; `sudo mkdir /beta` at the `$` prompt. Next, change the owner in the group to the `alpha` user. Enter the command; `sudo chown alpha:alpha /beta`. Relist the files in the `root` directory (see the following screenshot):

```
pi@Slv1:~ $ ls -la /
total 96
drwxr-xr-x 22 root root   4096 Sep  5 15:47 .
drwxr-xr-x 22 root root   4096 Sep  5 15:47 ..
drwxr-xr-x  2 alpha alpha 4096 Sep  5 15:47 beta
drwxr-xr-x  2 root root   4096 Sep  4 19:01 bin
drwxr-xr-x  3 root root  16384 Dec 31  1969 boot
drwxr-xr-x 15 root root   3500 Sep  5 01:07 dev
drwxr-xr-x 111 root root  4096 Sep  5 09:02 etc
drwxr-xr-x  4 root root   4096 Sep  5 09:01 home
drwxr-xr-x 19 root root   4096 Sep  4 19:01 lib
drwx------  2 root root  16384 May 27 07:43 lost+found
drwxr-xr-x  3 root root   4096 Sep  4 19:50 media
drwxr-xr-x  2 root root   4096 May 27 07:04 mnt
drwxr-xr-x  7 root root   4096 Sep  4 18:59 opt
dr-xr-xr-x 155 root root     0 Dec 31  1969 proc
drwx------  2 root root   4096 Sep  5 00:41 root
drwxr-xr-x 20 root root    700 Sep  5 01:07 run
drwxr-xr-x  2 root root   4096 Sep  4 20:23 sbin
drwxr-xr-x  2 root root   4096 May 27 07:04 srv
dr-xr-xr-x 12 root root      0 Dec 31  1969 sys
drwxrwxrwt 11 root root   4096 Sep  5 15:17 tmp
drwxr-xr-x 11 root root   4096 Sep  4 19:49 usr
drwxr-xr-x 11 root root   4096 May 27 07:50 var
```

You see now that the `beta` drive was created and set to the `alpha` user. Let's try to remount the drive. Re-enter the command; `sudo mount Mst0:/beta /beta`. You should not see any more errors. List the content of the `beta` drive:

```
pi@Slv1:~ $ ls -la /beta
total 8
drwxr-xr-x  2 alpha alpha 4096 Sep  5 15:47 .
drwxr-xr-x 22 root  root  4096 Sep  5 15:47 ..
```

You see that there is nothing in the drive. This is because you did not put anything in it yet. Let's do a little experiment. Switch over to the `alpha` user by entering the command; `su - alpha`, and change the directory to the `beta` directory, enter `cd /beta`. Create and edit a filename `testing.x`. Use the `vim` command; that is, enter the command; `vim testing.x`. Press *i*, and then write the phrase; `Two atomic explosions...`, then write and quit: `Esc :wq`. Relist the files in the beta drive (see the following screenshot):

```
alpha@Slv1:/beta $ ls -la
total 12
drwxr-xr-x  2 alpha alpha 4096 Sep  5 16:31 .
drwxr-xr-x 22 root  root  4096 Sep  5 15:47 ..
-rw-r--r--  1 alpha alpha   25 Sep  5 16:31 testing.x
```

We now see the newly created `testing.x` file. Read the file using the `cat` command (see highlighted text in the following screenshot):

```
alpha@Slv1:/beta $ cat testing.x
Two atomic explosions....

alpha@Slv1:/beta $
```

Enter exit and ssh into the master node `Mst0`, and list the files in the `beta` drive (see the following screenshot):

```
alpha@Slv1:/beta $ exit
logout
pi@Slv1:~ $ ssh Mst0
pi@mst0's password:

The programs included with the Debian GNU/Linux system are free software;
the exact distribution terms for each program are described in the
individual files in /usr/share/doc/*/copyright.

Debian GNU/Linux comes with ABSOLUTELY NO WARRANTY, to the extent
permitted by applicable law.
Last login: Mon Sep 5 17:02:14 2016 from slv1
pi@Mst0:~ $ ls -la /beta
total 12
drwxr-xr-x  2 alpha alpha 4096 Sep  5 17:14 .
drwxr-xr-x 22 root  root  4096 Sep  5 14:27 ..
-rw-r--r--  1 alpha alpha   26 Sep  5 17:14 testing.x
```

You also see the `testing.x` file in the `beta` drive on the master node. Read the content in the file using the `cat` command:

```
pi@Mst0:~ $ cat /beta/testing.x
Two atomic explosions....

pi@Mst0:~ $
```

You see the same content as before, which shows that the drive was successfully mounted. Let's go ahead and run the first real test using open MPI on both the master node and the slave1 node. First, list the files in the `home` directory:

```
pi@Mst0:~ $ ls
calc-pi    call-procs    Downloads MPI_08    Pictures      Templates
calc-pi1   call-procs.c  MPI_03.c  MPI_08_b  Public        update.sh
calc-pi1.c C_PI          MPI_04    MPI_08_b.c python_games  upgrade.sh
calc-pi2   C_PI.c        MPI_04.c  MPI_08.c  reboot.sh     Videos
calc-pi2.c Desktop       MPI_06    Music     shutdown.sh
calc-pi.c  Documents     MPI_06.c  ntwk_rst.sh ssh.sh
pi@Mst0:~ $
```

Here we see all the C programs and their executables. You now want to copy those files to your `beta` folder so that they can be accessed by all the nodes in your supercomputer. So let's once again change the user to `alpha`, using the; `su - alpha` command, and then change the directory to the `beta` directory by entering `cd /beta`. Create a new folder called `gamma` for storing all your future codes. Enter `mkdir gamma`. Re-list the files in `beta` (see the following screenshot), you can now see the `gamma` folder:

```
alpha@Mst0:/beta $ mkdir gamma
alpha@Mst0:/beta $ ls -la
total 16
drwxr-xr-x  3 alpha alpha 4096 Sep  5 19:35 .
drwxr-xr-x 22 root  root  4096 Sep  5 14:27 ..
drwxr-xr-x  2 alpha alpha 4096 Sep  5 19:35 gamma
-rw-r--r--  1 alpha alpha   26 Sep  5 17:14 testing.txt
```

Change the directory into the `gamma` directory using `cd gamma` and copy the codes from `home pi` to this new `code` folder. At the `alpha@Mst0:/beta/gamma $` prompt, enter the command `cp -a /home/pi/call-procs* ./`. The `cp` means copy. `-a` is an argument that uses the same permissions as the files we are copying from. The `*` means both the file and its executable. `./` signifies copy to this current folder. In this case, the `gamma` folder. Copy all your codes and their executables using this command. Now list the files to see if they were copied (see highlighted text in the following screenshot):

```
alpha@Mst0:~ $ cd /beta/gamma
alpha@Mst0:/beta/gamma $ ls -la
total 144
drwxr-xr-x 2 alpha alpha 4096 Sep 21 09:32 .
drwxr-xr-x 3 alpha alpha 4096 Sep  5 19:35 ..
-rwxr-xr-x 1 root  root  8944 Sep 12 22:40 calc-pi
-rwxr-xr-x 1 root  root  8944 Sep 12 17:29 calc-pi1
-rw------- 1 pi    pi    2188 Sep  7 15:15 calc-pi1.c
-rwxr-xr-x 1 root  root  8944 Sep 12 17:29 calc-pi2
-rw------- 1 pi    pi    2188 Sep  9 17:13 calc-pi2.c
-rw------- 1 pi    pi    2251 Sep 12 22:37 calc-pi.c
-rwxr-xr-x 1 alpha alpha 6956 Sep 18 11:49 call-procs
-rw-r--r-- 1 alpha alpha  747 Sep 18 11:46 call-procs.c
-rwxr-xr-x 1 alpha alpha 6664 Sep 18 12:48 C_PI
-rw-r--r-- 1 alpha alpha  664 Sep 18 12:48 C_PI.c
-rwxr-xr-x 1 alpha alpha 9128 Sep 12 17:38 MPI_04
-rw-r--r-- 1 pi    pi    1643 Sep 11 15:17 MPI_04.c
-rwxr-xr-x 1 alpha alpha 9128 Sep 12 17:38 MPI_06
-rw-r--r-- 1 pi    pi    1751 Sep 12 17:14 MPI_06.c
-rwxr-xr-x 1 alpha alpha 9128 Sep 17 19:58 MPI_08
-rwxr-xr-x 1 alpha alpha 9128 Sep 18 14:00 MPI_08_b
-rw-r--r-- 1 alpha alpha 2464 Sep 18 13:57 MPI_08_b.c
-rw-r--r-- 1 alpha alpha 2406 Sep 17 19:34 MPI_08.c
alpha@Mst0:/beta/gamma $
```

Excellent! The files are all there. So now go ahead and run the `call-procs` program on the master node (see the following screenshot). Again, the processes were called randomly. Each execution will produce a different sequence of processes:

```
alpha@Mst0:/beta/gamma $ mpiexec -n 4 call-procs
Calling process 1 out of 4 on Mst0
Calling process 2 out of 4 on Mst0
Calling process 3 out of 4 on Mst0
Calling process 0 out of 4 on Mst0
```

At this point, we will make a slight modification to the processor call command, whereby you can call the processes on, not only a single node, but any of the cores/processes in the cluster (master and slaves) to assist with computation. The command is as follows:

```
alpha@Mst0:/beta/gamma $ mpiexec -H Mst0,Mst0,Mst0,Mst0,Slv1,Slv1,Slv1,Slv1 call-procs
Calling process 0 out of 8 on Mst0
Calling process 3 out of 8 on Mst0
Calling process 4 out of 8 on Slv1
Calling process 6 out of 8 on Slv1
Calling process 7 out of 8 on Slv1
Calling process 5 out of 8 on Slv1
Calling process 1 out of 8 on Mst0
Calling process 2 out of 8 on Mst0
alpha@Mst0:/beta/gamma $
```

The `-H` signifies the host core you want to run your program on, followed by the hostname of the cores. Here, the command is calling all eight cores between the master and slave. Feel free to experiment by eliminating some of the cores/processes between the two nodes to see what happens. Let's now use this same command to instruct the cores on your two-node supercomputer to calculate π. Enter the following command (feel free to use a smaller number of iterations or intervals to reduce the initial processing time):

```
alpha@Mst0:/beta/gamma $ time mpiexec -H Mst0 MPI_08_b

############################################################

Master node name: Mst0

Enter the number of intervals:

300000

*** Number of processes: 1

    Calculated pi = 3.1415926535907133
          M_PI = 3.1415926535897931
    Relative Error = 0.0000000000009202

real    58m2.393s
user    57m50.110s
sys     0m0.270s




alpha@Mst0:/beta/gamma $ time mpiexec -H Mst0,Mst0 MPI_08_b

############################################################

Master node name: Mst0

Enter the number of intervals:

300000

*** Number of processes: 2

    Calculated pi = 3.1415926535907115
          M_PI = 3.1415926535897931
    Relative Error = 0.0000000000009184

real    29m24.936s
user    58m27.510s
sys     0m1.110s
```

```
alpha@Mst0:/beta/gamma $ time mpiexec -H Mst0,Mst0,Mst0 MPI_08_b

##########################################################

Master node name: Mst0

Enter the number of intervals:

300000

*** Number of processes: 3

    Calculated pi = 3.1415926535907026
           M_PI = 3.1415926535897931
    Relative Error = 0.0000000000009095

real    19m52.516s
user    58m49.690s
sys     0m1.800s



alpha@Mst0:/beta/gamma $ time mpiexec -H Mst0,Mst0,Mst0,Mst0 MPI_08_b

##########################################################

Master node name: Mst0

Enter the number of intervals:

300000

*** Number of processes: 4

    Calculated pi = 3.1415926535907128
           M_PI = 3.1415926535897931
    Relative Error = 0.0000000000009197

real    16m31.818s
user    63m8.070s
sys     0m2.090s
```

```
alpha@Mst0:/beta/gamma $ time mpiexec -H Mst0,Mst0,Mst0,Mst0,Slv1 MPI_08_b

#########################################################

Master node name: Mst0

Enter the number of intervals:

300000

*** Number of processes: 5

    Calculated pi = 3.1415926535907062
           M_PI = 3.1415926535897931
    Relative Error = 0.0000000000009130

real    19m58.245s
user    60m17.960s
sys     16m59.740s



alpha@Mst0:/beta/gamma $ time mpiexec -H Mst0,Mst0,Mst0,Mst0,Slv1,Slv1 MPI_08_b

#########################################################

Master node name: Mst0

Enter the number of intervals:

300000

*** Number of processes: 6

    Calculated pi = 3.1415926535907062
           M_PI = 3.1415926535897931
    Relative Error = 0.0000000000009130

real    17m24.661s
user    51m24.560s
sys     15m52.630s
```

 The temporary increase in processing time extant at the transition point (process 5) between the master and slave nodes (16m31.818s versus 19m58.245s), followed then by a gradual decrease in processing time as the sixth, seventh, and eight `Slv1` cores are successively brought online.

The elevated processing time at the transition point is, in fact, related to the latency between the communication ports in the switch. However, this problem becomes less of a factor with higher iteration values. This latency bugaboo is, indeed, a bane to high speed computing involving multiple nodes, and is a limiting factor for achieving the theoretical upper limit in supercomputing. Nonetheless, this problem can be mitigated by using state-of-the-art high speed switches:

```
alpha@Mst0:/beta/gamma $ time mpiexec -H Mst0,Mst0,Mst0,Mst0,Slv1,Slv1,Slv1 MPI_08_b

######################################################

Master node name: Mst0

Enter the number of intervals:

300000

*** Number of processes: 7

    Calculated pi = 3.1415926535907106
          M_PI = 3.1415926535897931
    Relative Error = 0.0000000000009175

real    15m39.574s
user    45m14.390s
sys     15m19.120s


alpha@Mst0:/beta/gamma $ time mpiexec -H Mst0,Mst0,Mst0,Mst0,Slv1,Slv1,Slv1,Slv1 MPI_08_b

######################################################

Master node name: Mst0

Enter the number of intervals:

300000

*** Number of processes: 8

    Calculated pi = 3.1415926535907150
          M_PI = 3.1415926535897931
    Relative Error = 0.0000000000009219

real    14m19.053s
user    41m10.760s
sys     14m32.330s
```

Summary

In this chapter, we learned how to create a mountable drive on the master node. To accomplish this task, we employed several Linux commands, such as `mkdir`, used for making an `export` drive folder, `chown`, used for changing ownership of the `export` drive from the `root` user to a new user, and `rpcbind`, which allowed the master Pi to export the MPI codes to the slave nodes. We also learned how to edit the `exports` file that was used to facilitate exporting the MPI codes on the master node to the slave nodes. We learned how to use the `nfs-kernel-server` command after editing the `exports` file. We edited the `rc.local` file, which is a bootup script, that was used to make the master node mountable. We learned how to use the `mount` command to manually mount the `export` drive containing the MPI codes, `cat` the command for displaying the contents of files, the `cp -a` command for copying files/codes to the `export` folder, and finally, the `-H` command, used to task any or all cores/nodes to work on a problem. In `Chapter 7`, *Configuring the Eight Nodes*, we will discuss how to configure the eight or sixteen nodes in your Pi supercomputer.

7
Configuring the Eight Nodes

This chapter discusses how to configure the eight or sixteen nodes in your Pi supercomputer. The process involves editing the `fstab`, `rc.local`, and `hosts` files. Additionally, you will be instructed on how to format the slave SD cards using the **SD formatter for Windows** applications and how to copy the slave1 SD card image, using the **win32 Disk Imager** application, to the remaining formatted slave SD cards.

In this chapter, you will learn:

- How to edit the `fstab` file on the slave1 node to set up an automatic mount command
- How to edit the boot up script `rc.local` file on the slave1 node for automatically mounting the export drive MPI code folder
- How to edit the `hosts` file on the master node and slave1 node to reflect, temporarily, the IP address and hostnames of the remaining six or fourteen slave nodes
- How to use the **SD formatter for Windows** applications to format the remaining slave SD cards
- How to use the **win32 Disk Imager** to copy the image of the Slave1 SD card from the main PC drive to the remaining slave SD cards.
- How to edit/update the `hosts` file on the remaining slave nodes to reflect their actual IP address
- How to edit the `interfaces` file on the super cluster nodes
- How to update the MAC and IP address on the network switch for the remaining slave nodes

Automating mounting of drives

We will now discuss the process of automating the mounting of the `gamma` drive. Enter exit, you should now be at the `pi@Mst0:~$`. Now `ssh` into the `slave` drive (`Slv1`). Enter the command; `sudo reboot`. After reboot, check to see if the `beta` folder was mounted (see the following screenshot):

```
pi@Slv1:~ $ ls -la /beta
total 8
drwxr-xr-x  2 alpha alpha 4096 Sep  5 15:47 .
drwxr-xr-x 22 root  root  4096 Sep  5 15:47 ..
```

Clearly, the `beta` drive did not mount. You therefore need to edit the `fstab` file, and set up an automatic mount point command in there, so that you don't have to execute the mount command every time somebody logs in after reboot. Enter the command; `sudo vim /etc/fstab` (see the following screenshot). Add the text highlighted in red:

```
proc            /proc       proc    defaults          0   0
/dev/mmcblk0p6  /boot       vfat    defaults          0   2
/dev/mmcblk0p7  /           ext4    defaults,noatime  0   1
# a swapfile is not a swap partition, no line here
#   use  dphys-swapfile swap[on|off]  for that

Mst0:/beta      /beta       nfs     defaults,rw,exec  0   0
```

The first argument `Mst0:/beta` is the same as the first argument used in the previous mount command (recall `Mst0` has the value of the IP address). The second argument `/beta` signifies the local drive you want to mount to. The third argument `nfs` is the type of filesystem being mounted to. The fourth argument is a series of parameters required for setting up the mount, and the last two arguments are simply zeros. Save this updated file by entering the command; `Esc :wq`. Next, you need to edit the boot up script `rc.local`. Enter the command; `sudo vim/etc/rc.local` (see the following screenshot):

```
#!/bin/sh -e
#
# rc.local
#
# This script is executed at the end of each multiuser runlevel.
# Make sure that the script will "exit 0" on success or any other
# value on error.
#
# In order to enable or disable this script just change the execution
# bits.
#
# By default this script does nothing.

# Print the IP address
_IP=$(hostname -I) || true
if [ "$_IP" ]; then
  printf "My IP address is %s\n" "$_IP"
fi

# Mount "beta" automatically

sleep 5
mount -a
exit 0
```

Add the text highlighted in red. The mount -a command automatically mounts the drive whenever the node boots up. The sleep 5 command is an added refinement to the system that temporarily delays boot up of the slave to give the master (Mst0) time to completely boot up, so that when the slave comes online, it will mount the exported beta drive from the master node. Enter Esc :wq. Relist the contents in the beta folder (see the following screenshot):

```
pi@Slv1:~ $ ls -la /beta
total 8
drwxr-xr-x  2 alpha alpha 4096 Sep  5 15:47 .
drwxr-xr-x 22 root  root  4096 Sep  5 15:47 ..
```

The beta drive has not mounted yet. Go ahead and enter; sudo mount -a, which is essentially same as the command in the boot script, and then relist the contents in beta.

```
pi@Slv1:~ $ ls -la /beta
total 16
drwxr-xr-x  3 alpha alpha 4096 Sep  5 19:35 .
drwxr-xr-x 22 root  root  4096 Sep  5 15:47 ..
drwxr-xr-x  2 alpha alpha 4096 Sep  5 19:54 gamma
-rw-r--r--  1 alpha alpha   26 Sep  5 17:14 testing.x
```

You should now see the `gamma` folder and `testing.x` files (see the preceding screenshot) if the drive correctly mounted. You can now test to see if the drive automatically mounts upon reboot. Go ahead and execute the command; `sudo reboot`, and then `ssh` back into `Slv1`. Relist the contents of `beta`. You should, once again, see the preceding screenshot. Let's run one more test. You want to make sure that files are mounted using the readable, writable, and executable permissions, so `ssh` back into `Mst0`, and change the user to the `alpha` user by using/entering the command; `su - alpha` (see the following screenshot):

```
pi@Mst0:~ $ su - alpha
Password:

* keychain 2.7.1 ~ http://www.funtoo.org
* Found existing ssh-agent: 1649
* Found existing gpg-agent: 1674
* Known ssh key: /home/alpha/.ssh/id_rsa

alpha@Mst0:~ $
```

Then change the directory to `gamma`, and then list the contents in `gamma` (see the following screenshot):

```
alpha@Mst0:~ $ cd /beta/gamma
alpha@Mst0:/beta/gamma $ ls -la
total 144
drwxr-xr-x 2 alpha alpha 4096 Sep 21 09:32 .
drwxr-xr-x 3 alpha alpha 4096 Sep 28 19:50 ..
-rwxr-xr-x 1 alpha alpha 6956 Sep 18 11:49 call-procs
-rw-r--r-- 1 alpha alpha  747 Sep 18 11:46 call-procs.c
-rwxr-xr-x 1 alpha alpha 6664 Sep 18 12:48 C_PI
-rw-r--r-- 1 alpha alpha  664 Sep 18 12:48 C_PI.c
-rwxr-xr-x 1 alpha alpha 9128 Sep 12 17:38 MPI_04
-rw-r--r-- 1 pi    pi    1643 Sep 11 15:17 MPI_04.c
-rwxr-xr-x 1 alpha alpha 9128 Sep 12 17:38 MPI_06
-rw-r--r-- 1 pi    pi    1751 Sep 12 17:14 MPI_06.c
-rwxr-xr-x 1 alpha alpha 9128 Sep 17 19:58 MPI_08
-rwxr-xr-x 1 alpha alpha 9128 Sep 18 14:00 MPI_08_b
-rw-r--r-- 1 alpha alpha 2464 Sep 18 13:57 MPI_08_b.c
```

You now see the requisite files. Go ahead now, and run one core on the master node, and one core on the slave node (see the following screenshot):

```
alpha@Mst0:/beta/gamma $ time mpiexec -H Mst0,Slv1 MPI_08_b

#############################################################

Master node name: Mst0

Enter the number of intervals:

100000


*** Number of processes: 2


    Calculated pi = 3.1415926535981162
            M_PI = 3.1415926535897931
    Relative Error = 0.0000000000083231

real    5m43.605s
user    4m12.070s
sys     1m23.770s
```

There were no errors. You can now effortlessly turn on your two-node supercomputer, and start running your favorite MPI programs. The next, and final step is finalizing the configuration of your eight or sixteen Pi supercomputer.

Setting up the host file for all nodes

Now that the first slave (Slv1) node is set up, you need to update the hosts file on both the master (Mst0) and slave (Slv1) nodes to reflect all the remaining six or sixteen nodes in the super cluster. First, you will copy (using **win32 Disk Imager**) the image of the Slv1 SD card to your desktop. This image file will then be copied to the other six or fourteen slave SD cards, and then return them to the slave Pis. Finally, you will make additional minor modifications to the data on each card.

So, let's now edit again the `hosts` file on the master node. Enter `exit` to return to the `pi@Mst0:~$` prompt, and then enter `sudo vim/etc/hosts`. Add the rest of the IP addresses and host names. Repeat this procedure for the slave (`Slv1`) node (see highlighted text in the following screenshot):

```
127.0.0.1     localhost
::1              localhost ip6-localhost ip6-loopback
ff02::1          ip6-allnodes
ff02::2          ip6-allrouters

#127.0.1.1     Slv1

192.168.0.9     Mst0
192.168.0.10    Slv1
192.168.0.11    Slv2
192.168.0.12    Slv3
192.168.0.13    Slv4
192.168.0.14    Slv5
192.168.0.15    Slv6
192.168.0.17    Slv7
```

Do the same for the master node, (see the following screenshot):

```
127.0.0.1     localhost
::1              localhost ip6-localhost ip6-loopback
ff02::1          ip6-allnodes
ff02::2          ip6-allrouters

# 127.0.1.1     Mst0

192.168.0.9     Mst0
192.168.0.10    Slv1
192.168.0.11    Slv2
192.168.0.12    Slv3
192.168.0.13    Slv4
192.168.0.14    Slv5
192.168.0.15    Slv6
192.168.0.16    Slv7
```

Note that those six additional records are place holders as the IP addresses for the remaining six slave nodes may change after energizing them so you might have to update these records after the slaves are energized. Energizing the slaves allows the Pis and switch to determine the additional new MAC and IP addresses, which you can then record, and subsequently update the `hosts` file accordingly. We will now discuss the process for copying the image of the `Slv1` SD card to the remaining slave cards.

Formatting the remaining slave SD cards

Before copying the image to the slave cards, you must first format them by using the
SD formatter for the Windows applications. So go ahead now and switch over to the
Windows environment. Download the **SD formatter for Windows** applications file from
the following website; `https://www.sdcard.org/downloads/formatter_4/eula_windows`
`/index.html`. Insert a loaded SD card adapter into the SD card drive slot on the main PC,
and double-click on the **applications** icon. Select the drive containing the SD card to be
formatted (in the authors case it was the `L` drive). Click on the **Option** button, and change
the settings as shown in the following screenshot. Click the **OK** button:

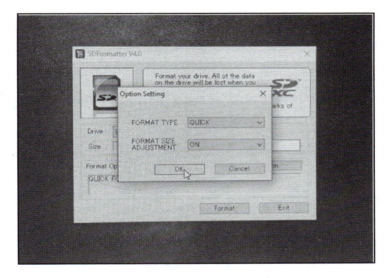

SD card formatter setting

Next, click on the **Format** button. The format process will take a few seconds. Repeat the process for the remaining slave cards:

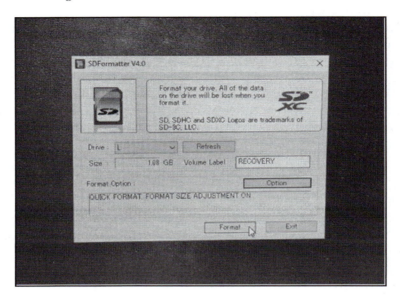

SD card formatter

We will now proceed to copy the `Slv1` image file to the six or fourteen formatted slave SD cards.

Copying the slave1 SD card image to the main computer drive

Now that the remaining six or fourteen slave cards are formatted, you will now copy the image of `Slv1` (using the **Win32 Disk Imager** application) to any reserve drive on the main computer, but first, download the file from the website; `https://sourceforge.net/projects/win32diskimager/`. If you are not currently on the slave node, `ssh` into it, and then execute; `sudo shutdown -h now`. Remove the SD card from the slave1 node, and insert it into the SD card slot on the main PC. Double-click on the **application** icon to install and/or execute the application (see the following screenshot). Select the SD device drive letter **N** from the **Device** option, where the card adapter was inserted (your drive letters may be different). Click the **folder** icon, and select the drive on which to save the image.

Give the file a name; for example, Slv1, and click the **open** button. You should now see a screen as shown in the following screenshot. Click **Read**. The application begins copying the image of Slv1 from the SD card in device drive N to the D drive on the author's main PC (this copying process takes several minutes). Upon completion of copying the disk image, return the card to its slave1 node:

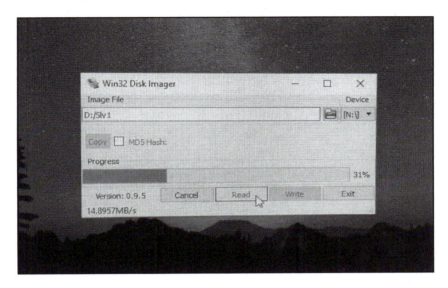

Win32 Disk Imager read

Copying the slave1 image to the remaining slave SD cards

We will now proceed to copy the Slv1 image to the other slave SD cards (see the following screenshot). Re-insert each of the remaining slave SD card into the SD slot on the main PC (the author is now using device drive **L** as the slave drive), and select, using the **folder**icon, the Slv1 file image now located on the D drive (the file does not appear in the window, so you must write in the name). Click the **open** button and then click the **Write** button as depicted in the following screenshot. The Slv1 image file is now being written to a remaining slave card.

The write process takes several minutes. Note that the author used two separate SD card drives, one was used as the source (device N) from which to copy the Slv1 image, and the other was the target (device L) for copying the Slv1 image from drive D. There is no rhyme nor reason for using different drives, you can use the same drive, it's just that device L accept the micro SD card, while device N accepted the SD card adapter:

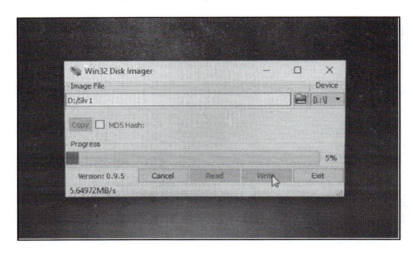

Win32 Disk Imager write

After the Slv1 file image has been written to all the remaining slave SD cards, reinsert each of them into their respective Pi node. Go ahead now and successively power on all the Pi2 or Pi3 nodes by inserting, one at a time, the Pis USB connector into the power brick. This will allow the Pis and the switch to learn the MAC and IP addresses of the remaining slave nodes. Next, return to the Pi monitor and update the slaves Hostname as per Chapter 3, *Preparing the Initial Two Nodes*. Ascertain (via ifconfig), and record the IP and MAC addresses of each remaining slave Pis. After acquiring this information go ahead and update the records (as you did earlier) in the hosts file for each slave Pi. You can update the hosts file either from the Pi monitor, or more conveniently, from the main PC (the author suggests the latter).

Go ahead now and reboot to the Ubuntu/Linux environment. `ssh` successively into the master, and slave nodes, and update their records in the `hosts` file, as depicted in the following screenshot. Note the new IP addresses of the remaining slave nodes just as the author predicted earlier:

```
127.0.0.1      localhost
::1            localhost ip6-localhost ip6-loopback
ff02::1        ip6-allnodes
ff02::2        ip6-allrouters

# 127.0.1.1   Mst0

192.168.0.9    Mst0
192.168.0.10   Slv1
192.168.0.18   Slv2
192.168.0.20   Slv3
192.168.0.22   Slv4
192.168.0.24   Slv5
192.168.0.25   Slv6
192.168.0.26   Slv7
```

Next, update the network `interfaces` file for all the six or fourteen slaves; that is, repeat the procedure outlined in Chapter 4, *Static IP Address and Hosts File Setup*. Also, update the switch's MAC and IP data to reflect the highlighted data depicted in the preceding screenshot; that is, repeat the procedure outlined in Chapter 4, *Static IP Address and Hosts File Setup*. You are now nearing the end of your arduous digital pilgrimage.

Summary

In this chapter, we learned how to configure the eight or sixteen nodes in your Pi supercomputer. We accomplished this task by initially editing the `fstab` file on the slave1 node to set up an automatic mount command, and then edit the `hosts` files on the master and slave nodes to reflect their temporary IP address. Next, we used the SD formatter for the Windows applications, to format the slave SD cards, and then the **win32 Disk Imager** application, to copy the slave1 image to the remaining formatted slave SD cards. We edited/updated the `hosts` file to reflect the actual IP addresses of the networked master and slaves, and edited the `interfaces` file on the super cluster nodes. Finally, we updated the MAC and IP address on the network switch for the remaining slave nodes. We will discuss testing the super cluster in Chapter 8, *Testing the Super Cluster*.

8
Testing the Super Cluster

This chapter discusses how to test the super cluster (see definition in `Appendix`). Initially, you will shut down the entire supercomputer by sequentially using the `shutdown -h now` command at each node, and then reenergize the super cluster to reinitialize the machine as it progresses through its start up sequence. After the nodes are up-and-running, you will then engage multiple nodes using the `-H` command to run/test the super cluster by eviscerating the time need to solve the π function. Finally, you will create `convenience bash` files to facilitate ease of use of your supercomputer.

In this chapter, you will learn:

- How to use the `shutdown -h now` command to shut down your Pis
- How to engage multiple cores/nodes, using the `-H` command, to solve the MPI π function in record time
- How to create `convenience bash` files for enhancing the user experience, while operating the supercomputer

Wielding the -H command

Shut down the entire cluster by successively **ssh**-ing into each node, and enter `sudo shutdown -h now` (we will discuss automating this procedure later). Reenergize the cluster by turning off the power strip, and then on again, or unplug the rapid charger from the wall socket, and then reinsert the plug into the socket. Wait about 30 seconds or so for the Pis to reboot. Then **ssh** into the master node, and switch to the `alpha` user, then change the directory to the `gamma` folder.

Execute the `call-procs` program to see if all the nodes are working appropriately. For example, if you have an eight or 16-node machine, type in, individually; `mpiexec -H Mst0 call-procs`, `mpiexec -H Slv1 call-procs`, `mpiexec -H Slv2 call-procs`, `mpiexec -H Slv3 call-procs`...`mpiexec -H Slv7 call-procs or Slv15 call-procs`. This procedure will initialize the nodes. Then command all the nodes using the command; `mpiexec -H Slv1,Slv2,Slv3,Slv4,Slv5,Slv6,Slv7,Slv8,Slv9,Slv10,Slv11,Slv12,Slv13,Slv14,Slv15 call-procs`. If all the nodes respond appropriately, then you are good to go. Have fun!

Fellow geeks, this is now the decisive moment. Rerun the command for testing the master, and slave Pi; that is, enter the command `time mpiexec -H Mst0,Mst0,Mst0,Mst0,Slv1,Slv1,Slv1,Slv1 MPI_08_b`. The runtime should be similar to your earlier runtime of approximately 14m19.05s, using 300,000 iterations in the restrained mode. After the run ends, run the nodes as shown on the following pages. Engaging the entire stack of eight Pi2s, should produce a run time of approximately 6m58.102s. If you observe this result, you have then achieved your goal of building a miniature supercomputer so be proud of your accomplishment. You have my permission to pop the Champagne cork now. You have just built your first eight or 16-node Raspberry Pi2 or Pi3 supercomputer. So, go ahead now, and wield your powerful -H scepter to demolish any or all mathematical enemies that stand in your path. Start with the runs depicted on the following pages.

Pi2 supercomputing

Execute the code MPI_08_b using 10, and then 12 nodes (see the following figure):

```
alpha@Mst0:/beta/gamma $ time mpiexec -H Mst0,Mst0,Mst0,Mst0,Slv1,Slv1,Slv1,Slv1,Slv2,Slv2
MPI_08_b

#######################################################

Master node name: Mst0

Enter the number of intervals:

300000

*** Number of processes: 10

    Calculated pi = 3.14159265359071726564366144848
          M_PI = 3.14159265358979311599796346854
    Relative Error = 0.00000000000009241496456979803

real    11m35.776s
user    32m36.770s
sys     11m52.790s


alpha@Mst0:/beta/gamma $ time mpiexec -H Mst0,Mst0,Mst0,Mst0,Slv1,Slv1,Slv1,Slv1,Slv2,Slv2,
Slv2,Slv2 MPI_08_b

#######################################################

Master node name: Mst0

Enter the number of intervals:

300000

*** Number of processes: 12

    Calculated pi = 3.14159265359072037426813039928
          M_PI = 3.14159265358979311599796346854
    Relative Error = 0.00000000000009272582701669307

real    10m34.038s
user    28m40.680s
sys     11m56.470s
```

Execute the code using 14, and then 16 nodes (see the following figure):

```
alpha@Mst0:/beta/gamma $ time mpiexec -H Mst0,Mst0,Mst0,Mst0,Slv1,Slv1,Slv1,Slv1,Slv2,Slv2,
Slv2,Slv2,Slv3,Slv3 MPI_08_b

####################################################

Master node name: Mst0

Enter the number of intervals:

300000

*** Number of processes: 14

    Calculated pi = 3.1415926535907194860897106999162
           M_PI = 3.1415926535897931159979634685544
    Relative Error = 0.0000000000009263700091747230617

real    10m32.910s
user    167971m35.280s
sys     81357m28.400s




alpha@Mst0:/beta/gamma $ time mpiexec -H Mst0,Mst0,Mst0,Mst0,Slv1,Slv1,Slv1,Slv1,Slv2,Slv2,
Slv2,Slv2,Slv3,Slv3,Slv3,Slv3 MPI_08_b

####################################################

Master node name: Mst0

Enter the number of intervals:

300000

*** Number of processes: 16

    Calculated pi = 3.1415926535907208183573402493492
           M_PI = 3.1415926535897931159979634685544
    Relative Error = 0.0000000000009277023593767808305

real    9m34.595s
user    24m17.770s
sys     12m36.530s
```

Execute the code using 18, and then 20 nodes (see the following figure):

```
alpha@Mst0:/beta/gamma $ time mpiexec -H Mst0,Mst0,Mst0,Mst0,Slv1,Slv1,Slv1,Slv1,Slv2,Slv2,
Slv2,Slv2,Slv3,Slv3,Slv3,Slv3,Slv4,Slv4 MPI_08_b

#########################################################

Master node name: Mst0

Enter the number of intervals:

300000

*** Number of processes: 18

    Calculated pi = 3.14159265359071993017892054922
           M_PI = 3.14159265358979311599979634685
    Relative Error = 0.0000000000009268141809570806

real    8m18.921s
user    21m4.740s
sys     10m55.560s



alpha@Mst0:/beta/gamma $ time mpiexec -H Mst0,Mst0,Mst0,Mst0,Slv1,Slv1,Slv1,Slv1,Slv2,Slv2,
Slv2,Slv2,Slv3,Slv3,Slv3,Slv3,Slv4,Slv4,Slv4,Slv4 MPI_08_b

#########################################################

Master node name: Mst0

Enter the number of intervals:

300000

*** Number of processes: 20

    Calculated pi = 3.14159265359072259471417964960
           M_PI = 3.14159265358979311599979634685
    Relative Error = 0.0000000000009294787162161810

real    7m48.721s
user    19m25.060s
sys     10m24.450s
```

Execute the code using 22, and then 24 nodes (see the following figure):

```
alpha@Mst0:/beta/gamma $ time mpiexec -H Mst0,Mst0,Mst0,Mst0,Slv1,Slv1,Slv1,Slv1,Slv2,Slv2,
Slv2,Slv2,Slv3,Slv3,Slv3,Slv3,Slv4,Slv4,Slv4,Slv4,Slv5,Slv5 MPI_08_b

#########################################################

Master node name: Mst0

Enter the number of intervals:

300000

*** Number of processes: 22


    Calculated pi = 3.14159265359072215062496979537
         M_PI = 3.14159265358979311597963468544
    Relative Error = 0.00000000000092903462700633093

real    7m47.741s
user    18m47.660s
sys     11m4.450s



alpha@Mst0:/beta/gamma $ time mpiexec -H Mst0,Mst0,Mst0,Mst0,Slv1,Slv1,Slv1,Slv1,Slv2,Slv2,
Slv2,Slv2,Slv3,Slv3,Slv3,Slv3,Slv4,Slv4,Slv4,Slv4,Slv5,Slv5,Slv5,Slv5 MPI_08_b

#########################################################

Master node name: Mst0

Enter the number of intervals:

300000

*** Number of processes: 24


    Calculated pi = 3.14159265359072126244655009412
         M_PI = 3.14159265358979311597963468544
    Relative Error = 0.00000000000092814644858663068

real    7m21.174s
user    17m37.090s
sys     10m35.160s
```

Execute the code using 26, and then 28 nodes (see the following figure):

```
alpha@Mst0:/beta/gamma $ time mpiexec -H Mst0,Mst0,Mst0,Mst0,Slv1,Slv1,Slv1,Slv1,Slv2,Slv2,
Slv2,Slv2,Slv3,Slv3,Slv3,Slv3,Slv4,Slv4,Slv4,Slv4,Slv5,Slv5,Slv5,Slv5,Slv6,Slv6 MPI_08_b

##########################################################

Master node name: Mst0

Enter the number of intervals:

300000

*** Number of processes: 26

    Calculated pi = 3.14159265359072081835734024349349
            M_PI = 3.14159265358979311599793468544
    Relative Error = 0.00000000000009277023593768080805

real    7m36.579s
user    17m31.840s
sys     11m29.320s



alpha@Mst0:/beta/gamma $ time mpiexec -H Mst0,Mst0,Mst0,Mst0,Slv1,Slv1,Slv1,Slv1,Slv2,Slv2,
Slv2,Slv2,Slv3,Slv3,Slv3,Slv3,Slv4,Slv4,Slv4,Slv4,Slv5,Slv5,Slv5,Slv5,Slv6,Slv6,Slv6,Slv6
MPI_08_b

##########################################################

Master node name: Mst0

Enter the number of intervals:

300000

*** Number of processes: 28

    Calculated pi = 3.14159265359072126244655099412
            M_PI = 3.14159265358979311599793468544
    Relative Error = 0.00000000000009281464485866330868

real    8m3.386s
user    17m50.720s
sys     12m36.570s
```

Execute the code using 30, and then 32 nodes (see the following figure):

```
alpha@Mst0:/beta/gamma $ time mpiexec -H Mst0,Mst0,Mst0,Mst0,Slv1,Slv1,Slv1,Slv1,Slv2,Slv2,
Slv2,Slv2,Slv3,Slv3,Slv3,Slv3,Slv4,Slv4,Slv4,Slv4,Slv5,Slv5,Slv5,Slv5,Slv6,Slv6,Slv6,Slv6,Slv7,
Slv7 MPI_08_b

#######################################################

Master node name: Mst0

Enter the number of intervals:

300000

*** Number of processes: 30

    Calculated pi = 3.1415926535907199301789205492224
         M_PI = 3.14159265358979311599797963468544
   Relative Error = 0.0000000000000926814180957080680

real    7m25.487s
user    16m26.870s
sys     11m44.520s



alpha@Mst0:/beta/gamma $ time mpiexec -H Mst0,Mst0,Mst0,Mst0,Slv1,Slv1,Slv1,Slv1,Slv2,Slv2,
Slv2,Slv2,Slv3,Slv3,Slv3,Slv3,Slv4,Slv4,Slv4,Slv4,Slv5,Slv5,Slv5,Slv5,Slv6,Slv6,Slv6,Slv6,Slv7,
Slv7,Slv7,Slv7 MPI_08_b

#######################################################

Master node name: Mst0

Enter the number of intervals:

300000

*** Number of processes: 32

    Calculated pi = 3.1415926535907203742681301399287
         M_PI = 3.14159265358979311599797963468544
   Relative Error = 0.0000000000000927258270166930743

real    6m58.102s
user    15m34.740s
sys     11m12.650s
alpha@Mst0:/beta/gamma $
```

The preceding runs were generated by the author's 8-node, 32 core, 32 GHz. Raspberry Pi2 supercomputer. If you are now feeling same as the all powerful Dr. Doom, and crave even more power at your fingertips, you can build an even faster machine by adding more Pi2s or the more advanced Pi3s.

Pi3 supercomputing

The following runs were generated by the author's 16-node, 64 core, 76.8 GHz. Raspberry Pi3 supercomputer. The runs clearly show the advantage of higher core processing speed, and greater node count. The following two images depict the author's beloved Pi3 supercomputer:

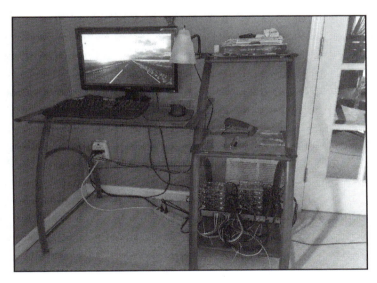

Author's 16-node, 64 cores, 76.8 GHz Raspberry Pi3 Supercomputer:

Close-up of the 16-node Raspberry Pi3 Supercomputer

Let's now have a look at the super cluster execution command syntax, and run results:

```
alpha@Mst0:/beta/gamma $ time mpiexec -H Mst0 MPI_08_b
######################################################

Master node name: Mst0

Enter the number of intervals:

300000


*** Number of processes: 1

    Calculated pi = 3.14159265359071326884072798285
            M_PI = 3.14159265358979311599796346854
    Relative Error = 0.000000000000920152842809329741

real 39m34.726s
user 39m25.120s
sys  0m0.120s
```

```
alpha@Mst0:/beta/gamma $ time mpiexec -H Mst0,Mst0 MPI_08_b
#######################################################

Master node name: Mst0

Enter the number of intervals:

300000


*** Number of processes: 2

      Calculated pi = 3.14159265359071149248393398034
              M_PI = 3.14159265358979311599796346854
     Relative Error = 0.00000000000091837648596992949

real  19m59.694s
user  39m47.750s
sys   0m0.410s



alpha@Mst0:/beta/gamma $ time mpiexec -H Mst0,Mst0,Mst0 MPI_08_b
#######################################################

Master node name: Mst0

Enter the number of intervals:

300000


*** Number of processes: 3

      Calculated pi = 3.14159265359070261069973639678
              M_PI = 3.14159265358979311599796346854
     Relative Error = 0.00000000000090949470177292823

real  13m30.216s
user  40m2.400s
sys   0m0.750s
```

```
alpha@Mst0:/beta/gamma $ time mpiexec -H Mst0,Mst0,Mst0,Mst0 MPI_08_b
########################################################

Master node name: Mst0

Enter the number of intervals:

300000


*** Number of processes: 4

    Calculated pi = 3.14159265359071282475156294822
            M_PI = 3.141592653589793115997963468544
    Relative Error = 0.00000000000091970875359947967

real  11m9.049s
user  42m41.770s
sys   0m0.780s
```

We will now transitioned to the second node or slave1, and, once again we see, from the run time (16m12.707s) depicted following, the effects of the switching latency between switching port 1, and port 2 or, more precisely, node 1 (master), and node 2 (slave1). Recall that there are four cores per processor. The author has commanded a fifth core, which is core 1 on slave1, to also work on the π equation.

Unfortunately, this latency problem will persist, and accumulate as you add more nodes that are locate at transition ports. The only solution to this issue is to use a faster switch. Currently, fast switches are prohibitively expensive for the hobbyist, or the common man. Indeed, only national governments, and large multi-billion dollar companies, and corporations can afford to play at the highest level in this supercomputing game as they voraciously pursue the holy grail of infinite processing speed. Infinite? Just kidding of course – no one really knows when or how the maddening quest ends. However, after observing the Pi2, and Pi3 runs, it is quite clear that the Pi3 supercomputer (with it more capable processors) significantly outperforms the Pi2.

The good news for hobbyist of a future generation, is that they will be able to build a relatively cheap supercomputer (provided the chip, and switching technology continue to advance) that will have the same processing power as today's super machines – similar to your current effort in building a Pi supercomputers that, in most instances, exceeds the processing power of yesteryear supercomputers.

One more item before we proceed. The author used the relatively cheap 16-port fiber optic cable capable `HP 1920-16G Managed Gigabit Switch` with his 16-node Pi3 supercomputer. This switch is a big brother to the 8-port HP managed switch used on his Pi2 supercomputer. Feel free to use any other brand of managed switch with your supercomputer, just make sure you carefully read the instructions on how to implement static MAC, and static IP configurations:

```
alpha@Mst0:/beta/gamma $ time mpiexec -H Mst0,Mst0,Mst0,Mst0,Slv1 MPI_08_b
#######################################################

Master node name: Mst0

Enter the number of intervals:

300000


*** Number of processes: 5

    Calculated pi = 3.14159265359070616341341519.7283
            M_PI = 3.14159265358979311599796346.8544
   Relative Error = 0.00000000000091304741545172.8739

real  16m12.707s
user  46m36.170s
sys   15m57.120s



alpha@Mst0:/beta/gamma $ time mpiexec -H Mst0,Mst0,Mst0,Mst0,Slv1,Slv1
MPI_08_b
#######################################################

Master node name: Mst0

Enter the number of intervals:

300000


*** Number of processes: 6

    Calculated pi = 3.14159265359070616341341519.7283
            M_PI = 3.14159265358979311599796346.8544
   Relative Error = 0.00000000000091304741545172.8739

real  14m7.660s
```

```
user  39m43.840s
sys   14m24.510s




alpha@Mst0:/beta/gamma $ time mpiexec -H Mst0,Mst0,Mst0,Mst0,Slv1,Slv1,Slv1
MPI_08_b
######################################################

Master node name: Mst0

Enter the number of intervals:

300000


*** Number of processes: 7

    Calculated pi = 3.14159265359071060430551369790 9
            M_PI = 3.14159265358979311599796346854 4
  Relative Error = 0.00000000000091748830755022936 5

real 12m26.877s
user 34m47.440s
sys   13m3.220s



alpha@Mst0:/beta/gamma $ time mpiexec -H
Mst0,Mst0,Mst0,Mst0,Slv1,Slv1,Slv1,
Slv1 MPI_08_b
######################################################

Master node name: Mst0

Enter the number of intervals:

300000
```

```
*** Number of processes: 8

     Calculated pi = 3.141592653590715045197612198535
             M_PI = 3.141592653589793115997963468544
    Relative Error = 0.000000000000921929199648729991

real 11m31.987s
user 31m52.810s
sys  12m36.590s
```

```
alpha@Mst0:/beta/gamma $ time mpiexec -H
Mst0,Mst0,Mst0,Mst0,Slv1,Slv1,Slv1,
Slv1,Slv2,Slv2 MPI_08_b
########################################################
```

```
Master node name: Mst0

Enter the number of intervals:

300000
```

```
*** Number of processes: 10

     Calculated pi = 3.141592653590717265643661448848
             M_PI = 3.141592653589793115997963468544
    Relative Error = 0.000000000000924149645697980304

real 9m27.184s
user 25m35.720s
sys  10m47.060s
```

```
alpha@Mst0:/beta/gamma $ time mpiexec -H
Mst0,Mst0,Mst0,Mst0,Slv1,Slv1,Slv1,
Slv1,Slv2,Slv2,Slv2,Slv2 MPI_08_b
########################################################
```

```
Master node name: Mst0

Enter the number of intervals:

300000


*** Number of processes: 12

     Calculated pi = 3.1415926535907203742268130399287
             M_PI = 3.1415926535897931159997963468544
    Relative Error = 0.0000000000009272582701669330743

real 8m49.813s
user 22m46.090s
sys  10m56.390s
```

```
alpha@Mst0:/beta/gamma $ time mpiexec -H
Mst0,Mst0,Mst0,Mst0,Slv1,Slv1,Slv1,
Slv1,Slv2,Slv2,Slv2,Slv2,Slv3,Slv3 MPI_08_b
###################################################

Master node name: Mst0

Enter the number of intervals:

300000


*** Number of processes: 14

     Calculated pi = 3.1415926535907194860897106991 62
             M_PI = 3.1415926535897931159997963468544
    Relative Error = 0.0000000000009263700917472306 17

real 7m41.531s
user 20m6.740s
sys  9m28.510s
```

```
alpha@Mst0:/beta/gamma $ time mpiexec -H
Mst0,Mst0,Mst0,Mst0,Slv1,Slv1,Slv1,
Slv1,Slv2,Slv2,Slv2,Slv2,Slv3,Slv3,Slv3,Slv3 MPI_08_b
####################################################

Master node name: Mst0

Enter the number of intervals:

300000


*** Number of processes: 16

    Calculated pi = 3.1415926535907208183357340249349
            M_PI = 3.1415926535897931159997963468544
   Relative Error = 0.0000000000009277023593767808055

real 7m5.758s
user 17m47.660s
sys  9m27.860s
```

```
alpha@Mst0:/beta/gamma $ time mpiexec -H
Mst0,Mst0,Mst0,Mst0,Slv1,Slv1,Slv1,
Slv1,Slv2,Slv2,Slv2,Slv2,Slv3,Slv3,Slv3,Slv3,Slv4,Slv4 MPI_08_b
####################################################

Master node name: Mst0

Enter the number of intervals:

300000


*** Number of processes: 18

    Calculated pi = 3.1415926535907199301789205492224
            M_PI = 3.1415926535897931159997963468544
   Relative Error = 0.0000000000009268141809570806800
```

```
real  6m12.352s
user  15m26.270s
sys   8m26.940s


alpha@Mst0:/beta/gamma $ time mpiexec -H
Mst0,Mst0,Mst0,Mst0,Slv1,Slv1,Slv1,
Slv1,Slv2,Slv2,Slv2,Slv2,Slv3,Slv3,Slv3,Slv3,Slv4,Slv4,Slv4,Slv4 MPI_08_b
######################################################

Master node name: Mst0

Enter the number of intervals:

300000


*** Number of processes: 20

    Calculated pi = 3.14159265359072259471417964960 0
             M_PI = 3.14159265358979311599796346854 4
    Relative Error = 0.00000000000092947871621618105 6

real  6m18.800s
user  15m6.500s
sys   9m11.310s
```

```
alpha@Mst0:/beta/gamma $ time mpiexec -H
Mst0,Mst0,Mst0,Mst0,Slv1,Slv1,Slv1,
Slv1,Slv2,Slv2,Slv2,Slv2,Slv3,Slv3,Slv3,Slv3,Slv4,Slv4,Slv4,Slv4,Slv5,Slv5
MPI_08_b
######################################################

Master node name: Mst0

Enter the number of intervals:
```

```
300000


*** Number of processes: 22

     Calculated pi = 3.14159265359072215062496979537
             M_PI = 3.14159265358979311599796346854
    Relative Error = 0.00000000000929034627006330993

real  5m40.196s
user  13m42.310s
sys   8m10.410s



alpha@Mst0:/beta/gamma $ time mpiexec -H
Mst0,Mst0,Mst0,Mst0,Slv1,Slv1,Slv1,
Slv1,Slv2,Slv2,Slv2,Slv2,Slv3,Slv3,Slv3,Slv3,Slv4,Slv4,Slv4,Slv4,Slv5,Slv5,
Slv5,Slv5 MPI_08_b
######################################################

Master node name: Mst0

Enter the number of intervals:

300000


*** Number of processes: 24

     Calculated pi = 3.14159265359072126244655099412
             M_PI = 3.14159265358979311599796346854
    Relative Error = 0.00000000000928146448586630868

real  5m51.449s
user  13m30.780s
sys   8m30.330s




alpha@Mst0:/beta/gamma $ time mpiexec -H
Mst0,Mst0,Mst0,Mst0,Slv1,Slv1,Slv1,
```

```
Slv1,Slv2,Slv2,Slv2,Slv2,Slv3,Slv3,Slv3,Slv3,Slv4,Slv4,Slv4,Slv4,Slv5,Slv5,
Slv5,Slv5,Slv6,Slv6 MPI_08_b
########################################################

Master node name: Mst0

Enter the number of intervals:

300000


*** Number of processes: 26

     Calculated pi = 3.14159265359072081835734O249349
             M_PI = 3.14159265358979311599796346B544
     Relative Error = 0.00000000000092770235937678080S

real 6m0.078s
user 13m27.300s
sys  9m10.070s



alpha@Mst0:/beta/gamma $ time mpiexec -H
Mst0,Mst0,Mst0,Mst0,Slv1,Slv1,Slv1,
Slv1,Slv2,Slv2,Slv2,Slv2,Slv3,Slv3,Slv3,Slv3,Slv4,Slv4,Slv4,Slv4,Slv5,Slv5,
Slv5,Slv5,Slv6,Slv6,Slv6,Slv6 MPI_08_b
########################################################

Master node name: Mst0

Enter the number of intervals:

300000


*** Number of processes: 28

     Calculated pi = 3.14159265359072126244655O099412
             M_PI = 3.14159265358979311599796346B544
     Relative Error = 0.0000000000009281464485866308SB

real 5m24.701s
user 12m31.440s
sys  8m15.760s
```

```
alpha@Mst0:/beta/gamma $ time mpiexec -H
Mst0,Mst0,Mst0,Mst0,Slv1,Slv1,Slv1,
Slv1,Slv2,Slv2,Slv2,Slv2,Slv3,Slv3,Slv3,Slv3,Slv4,Slv4,Slv4,Slv4,Slv5,Slv5,
Slv5,Slv5,Slv6,Slv6,Slv6,Slv6,Slv7,Slv7 MPI_08_b
######################################################

Master node name: Mst0

Enter the number of intervals:

300000


*** Number of processes: 30

      Calculated pi = 3.14159265359071993017892054 9224
              M_PI = 3.14159265358979311599796346 8544
    Relative Error = 0.00000000000092681418095708 0680

real 5m12.151s
user 11m34.040s
sys  8m24.120s



alpha@Mst0:/beta/gamma $ time mpiexec -H
Mst0,Mst0,Mst0,Mst0,Slv1,Slv1,Slv1,
Slv1,Slv2,Slv2,Slv2,Slv2,Slv3,Slv3,Slv3,Slv3,Slv4,Slv4,Slv4,Slv4,Slv5,Slv5,
Slv5,Slv5,Slv6,Slv6,Slv6,Slv6,Slv7,Slv7,Slv7,Slv7 MPI_08_b
######################################################

Master node name: Mst0

Enter the number of intervals:

300000


*** Number of processes: 32

      Calculated pi = 3.14159265359072037426813039 9287
              M_PI = 3.14159265358979311599796346 8544
    Relative Error = 0.00000000000092725827016693 0743

real 5m8.955s
user 11m23.230s
sys  8m13.930s
```

```
alpha@Mst0:/beta/gamma $ time mpiexec -H
Mst0,Mst0,Mst0,Mst0,Slv1,Slv1,Slv1,
Slv1,Slv2,Slv2,Slv2,Slv2,Slv3,Slv3,Slv3,Slv3,Slv4,Slv4,Slv4,Slv4,Slv5,Slv5,
Slv5,Slv5,Slv6,Slv6,Slv6,Slv6,Slv7,Slv7,Slv7,Slv7,Slv8,Slv8,Slv8,Slv8,Slv9,
Slv9,Slv9,Slv9,Slv10,Slv10,Slv10,Slv10,Slv11,Slv11,Slv11,Slv11,Slv12,Slv12,
Slv12,Slv12,Slv13,Slv13,Slv13,Slv13,Slv14,Slv14,Slv14,Slv14,Slv15,Slv15,Slv
15,Slv15 MPI_08_b
##########################################################

Master node name: Mst0

Enter the number of intervals:

300000


*** Number of processes: 64

    Calculated pi = 3.14159265359072037426813039287
    M_PI = 3.1415926535897931159979634685544
    Relative Error = 0.000000000000927258270166930743

real  3m51.196s
user  7m30.340s
sys   7m9.180s
```

You can further refine the user experience in operating the super cluster by coding simple convenience commands into bash files depicted on the following pages. Create the files/programs on the master node by entering the command; vim ~/xx.sh, replacing **xx** with an appropriate name, for example; update, upgrade, and so on. Then insert the text for each convenience bash command as depicted in the following figure, then save, and quit.

Execute the convenience programs using the bash commands. Note that the bash term should precede the filename, which begins with ~/. As the program runs its course, it will ask for the Pi2 or Pi3 password except for the ssh.sh file, whereby just enter exit, until you arrive at the appropriate node. This file might not be as useful to you, but you can play around with it, if you so desire. A word of caution, using the upgrade command after you've successfully configured your supercomputer, could result in changes to the internal settings of the Pi's operating system, and thus resulting in your machine not work as you intended. This would mean, unfortunately, that you will have to redo the entire effort. So use this command only if you have no other choice.

Creating bash files

Enter `vim ~/update.sh`, and edit the `~/update.sh` file as shown following, and then write and quit:

```
#!/bin/bash

ssh Slv7 'sudo update'
ssh Slv6 'sudo update'
ssh Slv5 'sudo update'
ssh Slv4 'sudo update'
ssh Slv3 'sudo update'
ssh Slv2 'sudo update'
ssh Slv1 'sudo update'
```

Execute the `convenience bash` file `~/update.sh` as depicted following:

`pi@Mst0:~ $ bash ~/update.sh` ç `bash` execution command.

Enter `vim ~/upgrade.sh`, and edit the `~/upgrade.sh` file as shown following, and then write and quit:

```
#!/bin/bash

ssh Slv7 'sudo upgrade'
ssh Slv6 'sudo upgrade'
ssh Slv5 'sudo upgrade'
ssh Slv4 'sudo upgrade'
ssh Slv3 'sudo upgrade'
ssh Slv2 'sudo upgrade'
ssh Slv1 'sudo upgrade'
```

Execute the `convenience bash` file `~/upgrade.sh` as depicted here:

`pi@Mst0:~ $ bash ~/upgrade.sh` ç `bash` execution command.

Enter `vim ~/shutdown.sh`, and edit the `~/shutdown.sh` file as shown following, and then write and quit:

```
#!/bin/bash

ssh Slv7 'sudo shutdown -h now'
ssh Slv6 'sudo shutdown -h now'
ssh Slv5 'sudo shutdown -h now'
ssh Slv4 'sudo shutdown -h now'
ssh Slv3 'sudo shutdown -h now'
ssh Slv2 'sudo shutdown -h now'
ssh Slv1 'sudo shutdown -h now'
```

Execute the `convenience bash` file `~/shutdown.sh` as depicted here:

`pi@Mst0:~ $ bash ~/shutdown.sh` ç `bash` execution command.

Enter `vim ~/reboot.sh`, and edit the `~/reboot.sh` file as shown following, and then write and quit:

```
#!/bin/bash

ssh Slv7 'sudo reboot'
ssh Slv6 'sudo reboot'
ssh Slv5 'sudo reboot'
ssh Slv4 'sudo reboot'
ssh Slv3 'sudo reboot'
ssh Slv2 'sudo reboot'
ssh Slv1 'sudo reboot'
```

Execute the `convenience bash` file `~/reboot.sh` as depicted here:

`pi@Mst0:~ $ bash ~/reboot.sh` ç `bash` execution command. Enter `vim ~/ssh.sh`, and edit the `~/ssh.sh` file as shown following:

```
#!/bin/bash

ssh Slv1
ssh Slv2
ssh Slv3
ssh Slv4
ssh Slv5
ssh Slv6
ssh Slv7
```

Execute the `convenience bash` file `~/ssh.sh` as depicted here:

`pi@Mst0:~ $ bash ~/ssh.sh` ç `bash` execution command.

Now that you have at your disposal a very muscular 32 or 64 core Pi2 or Pi3 supercomputer, go show-off its immense processing power by, once again, resolving the integral π equation you've been experimenting with, only this time use 1,000,000 iterations instead of 300,000. Note the change in the π accuracy, and execution time. One million iterations on the restrained 16-node Pi3, takes 23m35.096s to complete, and 0m11.381s (unrestrained), please see code fragment as shown following.

Note that 1,000,000 iterations on the Pi2 (restrained) takes considerably longer for a solution, and only seconds in the unrestrained mode. The author threw the full 76.8 GHz processing power of his Pi3 at the π equation using 5,000,000 iterations (restrained). It took 7.611hrs. of processing time – a rather rigorous exercise for the Pi3 supercomputer – to generate a very accurate π value.

Using unrestrained MPI code logic

From here on, you can unleash the full power of your machine by simply commenting out the restraining outer `for` loop statement, as shown following in the code fragment. Most MPI codes you will write will not necessarily have the `for` loop coding format, but most of the exercises in this book will use this type of coding structure.

The code fragment will allow unrestrained processing:

```
// for(total_iter = 1; total_iter < n; total_iter++) ç comment this line
{
   sum = 0.0;
//     width = 1.0 / (double)total_iter; // width of a segment ç comment
this
                                            line
   width = 1.0 / (double)n; // width of a segment ç use this line
//       for(i = rank + 1; i <= total_iter; i += numprocs) ç comment this
line
   for(i = rank + 1; i <= n; i += numprocs) ç use this line instead
   {
       x = width * ((double)i - 0.5); // x: distance to center of i(th)
segment
       sum += 4.0/(1.0 + x*x); // sum of individual segment height for a
given
                                 // rank
   }
```

Please revisit `Chapter 2`, *One Node Supercomputing,* for a refresher explanation on the nested `for` loop used to throttle the processing power of the super cluster.

Summary

In this chapter, we learned how to test your supercomputer by first shutting down the entire cluster by using the `shutdown -h now` command at each node, and then reenergizing the super cluster to reinitialize the machine. This procedure was then followed by commanding multiple nodes simultaneously to demolish the time needed to solve the π equation. Recall that one core on the master Pi2 node, operating in the restrained mode, and using 300,000 iterations, took 58m2.393s to calculate π, and 6m58.102s using all 32 cores in the eight node cluster, while the Pi3 supercomputer, also operating in the restrained mode, took `39m34.726s` to calculate π using one core, and only `5m8.955s` using 32 cores, and an insanely `3m51.196s` using all 64 cores on the 16 node Pi3 machine. The author leaves it up to the reader to determine the time needed to crunch the value of π using 5 million (5,000,000) iterations, and all 64 cores in the unrestrained Pi3 supercomputer. The result is even more insane than the 3m51.19s obtained earlier. Have fun!! Chapter 9, *Real-World Math Application*, will provide some real-world practice examples in math.

9
Real-World Math Application

We will now investigate four widely used math equations. Three of these equations are the trigonometric functions; sine, cosine, and tangent, and one is the natural log function. We will parallelize the Taylor series expansion of the trigonometric, and the natural log functions.

The form of the preceding equations lends themselves to easy parallelization, and hence we will be using the programming structure you previously experimented with. We will initially start with the serial representation of the functions, and then proceed to modify/convert said functions to their MPI versions. The *unrestrained* Pi supercomputer will quickly demolish these equations while using only a few processors. In fact, using the entire super cluster would be overkill in most of the following exercises – much like bringing a heavy machine gun to a fist fight, as they say, but the exercises serve to strengthen the reader's MPI programming skills – albeit employing only a small portion of the extensive MPI library. So, let's now proceed to have more fun programming our machine.

In this chapter, you will learn:

- How to write and run the serial Taylor series expansion `sine(x)` function
- How to write and run the MPI Taylor series expansion `sine(x)` function
- How to write and run the serial Taylor series expansion `cosine(x)` function
- How to write and run the MPI Taylor series expansion `cosine(x)` function
- How to write and run a `combination` serial Taylor series expansion `tangent(x)` function
- How to write and run the `combination` MPI Taylor series expansion `tangent(x)` function
- How to write and run the serial Taylor series expansion `ln(x)` function
- How to write and run the MPI Taylor series expansion `ln(x)` function

The codes were initially developed and debugged on the author's main PC. The `.c` files were subsequently SFTP over to the master node on his Pi3 super cluster where the codes were then compiled in the export `gamma` folder. The following runs were generated using only 16 of 64 processors on the author's Pi3 supercomputer. Proceed to doing the upcoming exercises.

MPI Taylor series sine(x) function

Start with the following Taylor series `sine(x)` function:

$$\text{sine}(x) = \sum_{k=0}^{\infty} (-1^k) \times \frac{x^{2k+1}}{(2k+1)!}$$

On the master node, write, compile, and run this serial `sine(x)` code (see the following screenshot, which shows `serial sine(x)` code) to get a feel of the program:

```
/*********************************
 * Serial sine(x) code.          *
 *                               *
 * Taylor series representation  *
 * of the trigonometric sine(x). *
 *                               *
 * Author: Carlos R. Morrison    *
 *                               *
 * Date: 1/10/2017               *
 *********************************/
#include <math.h>
#include <stdio.h>
int main(void)
{
   unsigned int j;
   unsigned long int k;
   long long int B,D;
   int num_loops = 17;
   float y;
   double x;
   double sum0=0,A,C,E;
/************************************************************/
   printf("\n");
   printf("Enter angle(deg.):\n");
   printf("\n");
```

```
   scanf("%f",&y);
   if(y <= 180.0)
   {
      x = y*(M_PI/180.0);
   }
   else
   x = -(360.0-y)*(M_PI/180.0);
/*********************************************************/
   sum0 = 0;
   for(k = 0; k < num_loops; k++)
   {
      A = (double)pow(-1,k);// (-1^k)
      B = 2*k+1;
      C = (double)pow(x,B);// x^(2k+1)

      D = 1;
      for(j=1; j <= B; j++)// (2k+1)!
      {
         D *= j;
      }

      E = (A*C)/(double)D;

      sum0 += E;
   }// End of for(k = 0; k < num_loops; k++)

   printf("\n");
   printf(" %.1f deg. = %.3f rads\n", y, x);
   printf("Sine(%.1f) = %.4f\n", y, sum0);
   return 0;
}
```

Next, write, compile, and run the MPI version of the preceding serial `sine(x)` code (see the following `MPI sine(x)` code), using one processor from each of the 16 nodes:

```
/********************************
 * MPI sine(x) code.           *
 *                             *
 * Taylor series representation *
 * of the trigonometric sine(x). *
 *                             *
 * Author: Carlos R. Morrison  *
 *                             *
 * Date: 1/10/2017             *
 ********************************/
#include <mpi.h>  // (Open)MPI library
#include <math.h> // math library
```

```c
#include <stdio.h>// Standard Input/Output library

int main(int argc, char*argv[])
{
  long long int total_iter,B,D;
  int n = 17,rank,length,numprocs,i,j;
  unsigned long int k;
  double sum,sum0,rank_integral,A,C,E;
  float y,x;
  char hostname[MPI_MAX_PROCESSOR_NAME];

  MPI_Init(&argc, &argv);                      // initiates MPI
  MPI_Comm_size(MPI_COMM_WORLD, &numprocs);  // acquire number of processes
  MPI_Comm_rank(MPI_COMM_WORLD, &rank);       // acquire current process id
  MPI_Get_processor_name(hostname, &length); // acquire hostname

  if (rank == 0)
  {
    printf("\n");
    printf("####################################################");
    printf("\n\n");
    printf("*** Number of processes: %d\n",numprocs);
    printf("*** processing capacity: %.1f GHz.\n",numprocs*1.2);
    printf("\n\n");
    printf("Master node name: %s\n", hostname);
    printf("\n");
    printf("Enter angle(deg.):\n");
    printf("\n");
    scanf("%f",&y);
    if(y <= 180.0)
    {
      x = y*(M_PI/180.0);
    }
    else
    x = -(360.0-y)*(M_PI/180.0);
  }

// broadcast to all processes, the number of segments you want
  MPI_Bcast(&n, 1, MPI_INT, 0, MPI_COMM_WORLD);
  MPI_Bcast(&x, 1, MPI_INT, 0, MPI_COMM_WORLD);

// this loop increments the maximum number of iterations, thus providing
// additional work for testing computational speed of the processors
// for(total_iter = 1; total_iter < n; total_iter++)
  {
    sum0 = 0.0;
//    for(i = rank + 1; i <= total_iter; i += numprocs)
    for(i = rank + 1; i <= n; i += numprocs)
```

```
      {
        k  =  (i-1);
        A  =  (double)pow(-1,k);// (-1^k)
        B  =  2*k+1;
        C  =  (double)pow(x,B);// x^(2k+1)
        D  =  1;
        for(j=1;  j <= B;  j++)// (2k+1)!
        {
          D  *= j;
        }
        E  =  (A*C)/(double)D;
        sum0  += E;
      }

     rank_integral = sum0;// Partial sum for a given rank
//   collect and add the partial sum0 values from all processes
     MPI_Reduce(&rank_integral, &sum, 1, MPI_DOUBLE,MPI_SUM, 0,
     MPI_COMM_WORLD);

   }// End of for(total_iter = 1; total_iter < n; total_iter++)

   if(rank == 0)
   {
     printf("\n\n");
     printf("  %.1f deg. = %.3f rads\n", y, x);
     printf("Sine(%.3f) = %.3f\n", x, sum);
   }

// clean up, done with MPI
   MPI_Finalize();

   return 0;
}// End of int main(int argc, char*argv[])
```

Let's have a look at the MPI `sine(x)` run:

```
alpha@Mst0:/beta/gamma $ time mpiexec -H
Mst0,Slv1,Slv2,Slv3,Slv4,Slv5,Slv6,Slv7,Slv8,
Slv9,Slv10,Slv11,Slv12,Slv13,Slv14,Slv15 MPI_sine
#######################################################

*** Number of processes: 16
*** processing capacity: 19.2 GHz.


Master node name: Mst0

Enter angle(deg.):
```

```
0


    0.0 deg. = 0.000 rads
Sine(0.000) = 0.000

real  0m10.404s
user  0m1.290s
sys   0m0.280s




alpha@Mst0:/beta/gamma $ time mpiexec -H
Mst0,Slv1,Slv2,Slv3,Slv4,Slv5,Slv6,Slv7,Slv8,
Slv9,Slv10,Slv11,Slv12,Slv13,Slv14,Slv15 MPI_sine
####################################################

*** Number of processes: 16
*** processing capacity: 19.2 GHz.


Master node name: Mst0

Enter angle(deg.):
30


  30.0 deg. = 0.524 rads
Sine(0.524) = 0.500

real  0m11.621s
user  0m1.270s
sys   0m0.330s


alpha@Mst0:/beta/gamma $ time mpiexec -H
Mst0,Slv1,Slv2,Slv3,Slv4,Slv5,Slv6,Slv7,Slv8,
Slv9,Slv10,Slv11,Slv12,Slv13,Slv14,Slv15 MPI_sine
####################################################

*** Number of processes: 16
*** processing capacity: 19.2 GHz.


Master node name: Mst0

Enter angle(deg.):
```

```
60


   60.0 deg.  = 1.047 rads
Sine(1.047) = 0.866

real  0m6.494s
user  0m1.230s
sys   0m0.340s



alpha@Mst0:/beta/gamma $ time mpiexec -H
Mst0,Slv1,Slv2,Slv3,Slv4,Slv5,Slv6,Slv7,Slv8,
Slv9,Slv10,Slv11,Slv12,Slv13,Slv14,Slv15 MPI_sine
#####################################################

*** Number of processes: 16
*** processing capacity: 19.2 GHz.


Master node name: Mst0

Enter angle(deg.):

90


   90.0 deg.  = 1.571 rads
Sine(1.571) = 1.000

real  0m10.090s
user  0m1.200s
sys   0m0.380s



alpha@Mst0:/beta/gamma $ time mpiexec -H
Mst0,Slv1,Slv2,Slv3,Slv4,Slv5,Slv6,Slv7,Slv8,
Slv9,Slv10,Slv11,Slv12,Slv13,Slv14,Slv15 MPI_sine
#####################################################

*** Number of processes: 16
*** processing capacity: 19.2 GHz.


Master node name: Mst0

Enter angle(deg.):
```

```
120


  120.0 deg. = 2.094 rads
Sine(2.094) = 0.866

real 0m4.674s
user 0m1.220s
sys  0m0.370s



alpha@Mst0:/beta/gamma $ time mpiexec -H
Mst0,Slv1,Slv2,Slv3,Slv4,Slv5,Slv6,Slv7,Slv8,
Slv9,Slv10,Slv11,Slv12,Slv13,Slv14,Slv15 MPI_sine
#######################################################

*** Number of processes: 16
*** processing capacity: 19.2 GHz.


Master node name: Mst0

Enter angle(deg.):

150


  150.0 deg. = 2.618 rads
Sine(2.618) = 0.500

real 0m6.942s
user 0m1.240s
sys  0m0.360s




alpha@Mst0:/beta/gamma $ time mpiexec -H
Mst0,Slv1,Slv2,Slv3,Slv4,Slv5,Slv6,Slv7,Slv8,
Slv9,Slv10,Slv11,Slv12,Slv13,Slv14,Slv15 MPI_sine
#######################################################

*** Number of processes: 16
*** processing capacity: 19.2 GHz.
```

```
Master node name: Mst0

Enter angle(deg.):

180


  180.0 deg. = 3.142 rads
Sine(3.142) = 0.007

real  0m7.757s
user  0m1.190s
sys   0m0.370s




alpha@Mst0:/beta/gamma $ time mpiexec -H
Mst0,Slv1,Slv2,Slv3,Slv4,Slv5,Slv6,Slv7,Slv8,
Slv9,Slv10,Slv11,Slv12,Slv13,Slv14,Slv15 MPI_sine
#######################################################

*** Number of processes: 16
*** processing capacity: 19.2 GHz.


Master node name: Mst0

Enter angle(deg.):

210


  210.0 deg. = -2.618 rads
Sine(-2.618) = -0.500

real  0m9.312s
user  0m1.280s
sys   0m0.480s




alpha@Mst0:/beta/gamma $ time mpiexec -H
Mst0,Slv1,Slv2,Slv3,Slv4,Slv5,Slv6,Slv7,Slv8,
Slv9,Slv10,Slv11,Slv12,Slv13,Slv14,Slv15 MPI_sine
#######################################################
```

```
*** Number of processes: 16
*** processing capacity: 19.2 GHz.


Master node name: Mst0

Enter angle(deg.):

240


   240.0 deg. = -2.094 rads
Sine(-2.094) = -0.866

real  0m7.053s
user  0m1.300s
sys   0m0.320s




alpha@Mst0:/beta/gamma $ time mpiexec -H
Mst0,Slv1,Slv2,Slv3,Slv4,Slv5,Slv6,Slv7,Slv8,
Slv9,Slv10,Slv11,Slv12,Slv13,Slv14,Slv15 MPI_sine
#######################################################

*** Number of processes: 16
*** processing capacity: 19.2 GHz.


Master node name: Mst0

Enter angle(deg.):

270


   270.0 deg. = -1.571 rads
Sine(-1.571) = -1.000

real  0m9.521s
user  0m1.220s
sys   0m0.340s
```

```
alpha@Mst0:/beta/gamma $ time mpiexec -H
Mst0,Slv1,Slv2,Slv3,Slv4,Slv5,Slv6,Slv7,Slv8,
Slv9,Slv10,Slv11,Slv12,Slv13,Slv14,Slv15 MPI_sine
########################################################

*** Number of processes: 16
*** processing capacity: 19.2 GHz.


Master node name: Mst0

Enter angle(deg.):

300


  300.0 deg. = -1.047 rads
Sine(-1.047) = -0.866

real 0m20.375s
user 0m1.260s
sys  0m0.330s



alpha@Mst0:/beta/gamma $ time mpiexec -H
Mst0,Slv1,Slv2,Slv3,Slv4,Slv5,Slv6,Slv7,Slv8,
Slv9,Slv10,Slv11,Slv12,Slv13,Slv14,Slv15 MPI_sine
########################################################

*** Number of processes: 16
*** processing capacity: 19.2 GHz.


Master node name: Mst0

Enter angle(deg.):

330


  330.0 deg. = -0.524 rads
Sine(-0.524) = -0.500

real 0m7.629s
user 0m1.440s
sys  0m0.350s
```

```
alpha@Mst0:/beta/gamma $ time mpiexec -H
Mst0,Slv1,Slv2,Slv3,Slv4,Slv5,Slv6,Slv7,Slv8,
Slv9,Slv10,Slv11,Slv12,Slv13,Slv14,Slv15 MPI_sine
####################################################

*** Number of processes: 16
*** processing capacity: 19.2 GHz.


Master node name: Mst0

Enter angle(deg.):

360


  360.0 deg. = -0.000 rads
Sine(-0.000) = 0.000

real 0m11.463s
user 0m1.260s
sys  0m0.290s
```

The following figure is a plot of the MPI `sine(x)` run:

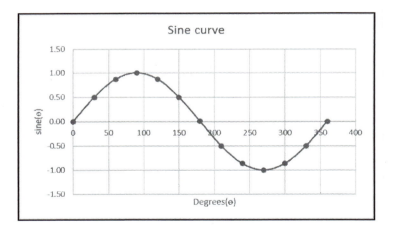

MPI Taylor series cosine(x) function

The Taylor series formula for the `cosine(x)` function is as follows:

$$\text{cosine}(x) = \sum_{k=0}^{\infty} (-1^k) \times \frac{x^{2k}}{(2k)!}$$

Write, compile, and run this `serial cosine(x)` code (see the following code, which shows `serial cosine(x)` code) to get a feel of the program:

```
/**********************************
\*  Serial cosine(x)code.        *
 *                               *
 *  Taylor series representation *
 *  of the trigonometric cosine(x).*
 *                               *
 *  Author: Carlos R. Morrison   *
 *                               *
 *  Date: 1/10/2017              *
 ********************************/
#include <math.h>
#include <stdio.h>

int main(void)
{
  unsigned int j;
  unsigned long int k;
  long long int B,D;
  int num_loops = 17;
  float y;
  double x;
  double sum0=0,A,C,E;
/*********************************************************/
  printf("\n");
  printf("Enter angle(deg.):\n");
  printf("\n");
  scanf("%f",&y);
  if(y <= 180.0)
  {
     x = y*(M_PI/180.0);
  }
  else
  x = -(360.0-y)*(M_PI/180.0);
/*********************************************************/
```

```
   sum0 = 0;
   for(k = 0; k < num_loops; k++)
   {
      A = (double)pow(-1,k);// (-1^k)
      B = 2*k;
      C = (double)pow(x,B);// x^2k

      D = 1;
      for(j=1; j <= B; j++)// (2k!)
      {
         D *= j;
      }

      E = (A*C)/(double)D;

      sum0 += E;
   }

   printf("\n");
   printf("    %.1f deg. = %.3f rads\n", y, x);
   printf("Cosine(%.1f) = %.4f\n", y, sum0);

   return 0;
}
```

Next, write, compile, and run the MPI version of the preceding serial cosine(x) code (see MPI cosine(x) code below), using one processor from each of the 16 nodes.

```
/**********************************
 * MPI cosine(x) code.            *
 *                                *
 * Taylor series representation   *
 * of the trigonometric cosine(x).*
 *                                *
 * Author: Carlos R. Morrison     *
 *                                *
 * Date: 1/10/2017                *
 **********************************/
#include<mpi.h>// (Open)MPI library
#include<math.h>// math library
#include<stdio.h>// Standard Input/Output library

int main(int argc, char*argv[])
{
   long long int total_iter,B,D;
   int n = 17,rank,length,numprocs,i,j;
   unsigned long int k;
   double sum,sum0,rank_integral,A,C,E;
```

```
    float y,x;
    char hostname[MPI_MAX_PROCESSOR_NAME];

    MPI_Init(&argc, &argv);                      // initiates MPI
    MPI_Comm_size(MPI_COMM_WORLD, &numprocs);    // acquire number of processes
    MPI_Comm_rank(MPI_COMM_WORLD, &rank);        // acquire current process id
    MPI_Get_processor_name(hostname, &length);   // acquire hostname

    if (rank == 0)
    {
      printf("\n");
      printf("###########################################################");
      printf("\n\n");
      printf("*** Number of processes: %d\n",numprocs);
      printf("*** processing capacity: %.1f GHz.\n",numprocs*1.2);
      printf("\n\n");
      printf("Master node name: %s\n", hostname);
      printf("\n");
      printf("Enter angle(deg.):\n");
      printf("\n");
      scanf("%f",&y);
      if(y <= 180.0)
      {
        x = y*(M_PI/180.0);
      }
      else
      x = -(360.0-y)*(M_PI/180.0);
    }

// broadcast to all processes, the number of segments you want
    MPI_Bcast(&n, 1, MPI_INT, 0, MPI_COMM_WORLD);
    MPI_Bcast(&x, 1, MPI_INT, 0, MPI_COMM_WORLD);

// this loop increments the maximum number of iterations, thus providing
// additional work for testing computational speed of the processors
//for(total_iter = 1; total_iter < n; total_iter++)
    {
      sum0 = 0.0;
//    for(i = rank + 1; i <= total_iter; i += numprocs)
      for(i = rank + 1; i <= n; i += numprocs)
      {
        k = (i-1);

        A = (double)pow(-1,k);// (-1^k)
        B = 2*k;
        C = (double)pow(x,B);// x^2k

        D = 1;
```

```
        for(j=1; j <= B; j++)// (2k!)
        {
          D *= j;
        }
        E = (A*C)/(double)D;

        sum0 += E;
      }

      rank_integral = sum0;// Partial sum for a given rank

//   collect and add the partial sum0 values from all processes
     MPI_Reduce(&rank_integral, &sum, 1, MPI_DOUBLE,MPI_SUM, 0,
     MPI_COMM_WORLD);

  }// End of for(total_iter = 1; total_iter < n; total_iter++)

  if(rank == 0)
  {
    printf("\n\n");
    printf("    %.1f deg. = %.3f rads\n", y, x);
    printf("Cosine(%.3f) = %.3f\n", x, sum);
  }
// clean up, done with MPI
  MPI_Finalize();

  return 0;
}// End of int main(int argc, char*argv[])
```

The following is the MPI cosine(*x*) run:

```
alpha@Mst0:/beta/gamma $ time mpiexec -H
Mst0,Slv1,Slv2,Slv3,Slv4,Slv5,Slv6,Slv7,Slv8,
Slv9,Slv10,Slv11,Slv12,Slv13,Slv14,Slv15 MPI_cosine
#######################################################

*** Number of processes: 16
*** processing capacity: 19.2 GHz.


Master node name: Mst0

Enter angle(deg.):

0

    0.0 deg. = 0.000 rads
```

```
Cosine(0.000) = 1.000

real  0m5.309s
user  0m1.280s
sys   0m0.280s



alpha@Mst0:/beta/gamma $ time mpiexec -H
Mst0,Slv1,Slv2,Slv3,Slv4,Slv5,Slv6,Slv7,Slv8,
Slv9,Slv10,Slv11,Slv12,Slv13,Slv14,Slv15 MPI_cosine
#######################################################

*** Number of processes: 16
*** processing capacity: 19.2 GHz.


Master node name: Mst0

Enter angle(deg.):

30

    30.0 deg. = 0.524 rads
Cosine(0.524) = 0.866



real  0m13.045s
user  0m1.270s
sys   0m0.400s



alpha@Mst0:/beta/gamma $ time mpiexec -H
Mst0,Slv1,Slv2,Slv3,Slv4,Slv5,Slv6,Slv7,Slv8,
Slv9,Slv10,Slv11,Slv12,Slv13,Slv14,Slv15 MPI_cosine
#######################################################

*** Number of processes: 16
*** processing capacity: 19.2 GHz.


Master node name: Mst0

Enter angle(deg.):

60
```

```
      60.0 deg. = 1.047 rads
Cosine(1.047) = 0.500

real  0m18.477s
user  0m1.150s
sys   0m0.450s


alpha@Mst0:/beta/gamma $ time mpiexec -H
Mst0,Slv1,Slv2,Slv3,Slv4,Slv5,Slv6,Slv7,Slv8,
Slv9,Slv10,Slv11,Slv12,Slv13,Slv14,Slv15 MPI_cosine
#####################################################

*** Number of processes: 16
*** processing capacity: 19.2 GHz.


Master node name: Mst0

Enter angle(deg.):

90


      90.0 deg. = 1.571 rads
Cosine(1.571) = -0.000

real  0m10.567s
user  0m1.240s
sys   0m0.360s

alpha@Mst0:/beta/gamma $ time mpiexec -H
Mst0,Slv1,Slv2,Slv3,Slv4,Slv5,Slv6,Slv7,Slv8,
Slv9,Slv10,Slv11,Slv12,Slv13,Slv14,Slv15 MPI_cosine
#####################################################

*** Number of processes: 16
*** processing capacity: 19.2 GHz.


Master node name: Mst0

Enter angle(deg.):

120


   120.0 deg. = 2.094 rads
```

```
Cosine(2.094) = -0.500

real  0m7.056s
user  0m1.310s
sys   0m0.330s



alpha@Mst0:/beta/gamma $ time mpiexec -H
Mst0,Slv1,Slv2,Slv3,Slv4,Slv5,Slv6,Slv7,Slv8,
Slv9,Slv10,Slv11,Slv12,Slv13,Slv14,Slv15 MPI_cosine
#####################################################

*** Number of processes: 16
*** processing capacity: 19.2 GHz.


Master node name: Mst0

Enter angle(deg.):

150


    150.0 deg. = 2.618 rads
Cosine(2.618) = -0.866

real  0m8.202s
user  0m1.200s
sys   0m0.390s




alpha@Mst0:/beta/gamma $ time mpiexec -H
Mst0,Slv1,Slv2,Slv3,Slv4,Slv5,Slv6,Slv7,Slv8,
Slv9,Slv10,Slv11,Slv12,Slv13,Slv14,Slv15 MPI_cosine
#####################################################

*** Number of processes: 16
*** processing capacity: 19.2 GHz.


Master node name: Mst0

Enter angle(deg.):
```

```
180


    180.0 deg. = 3.142 rads
Cosine(3.142) = -1.001

real  0m11.139s
user  0m1.250s
sys   0m0.350s



alpha@Mst0:/beta/gamma $ time mpiexec -H
Mst0,Slv1,Slv2,Slv3,Slv4,Slv5,Slv6,Slv7,Slv8,
Slv9,Slv10,Slv11,Slv12,Slv13,Slv14,Slv15 MPI_cosine
######################################################

*** Number of processes: 16
*** processing capacity: 19.2 GHz.


Master node name: Mst0

Enter angle(deg.):

210


    210.0 deg. = -2.618 rads
Cosine(-2.618) = -0.866

real  0m6.400s
user  0m1.290s
sys   0m0.330s




alpha@Mst0:/beta/gamma $ time mpiexec -H
Mst0,Slv1,Slv2,Slv3,Slv4,Slv5,Slv6,Slv7,Slv8,
Slv9,Slv10,Slv11,Slv12,Slv13,Slv14,Slv15 MPI_cosine
######################################################

*** Number of processes: 16
*** processing capacity: 19.2 GHz.
```

```
Master node name: Mst0

Enter angle(deg.):

240


    240.0 deg. = -2.094 rads
Cosine(-2.094) = -0.500

real  0m11.837s
user  0m1.320s
sys   0m0.340s



alpha@Mst0:/beta/gamma $ time mpiexec -H
Mst0,Slv1,Slv2,Slv3,Slv4,Slv5,Slv6,Slv7,Slv8,
Slv9,Slv10,Slv11,Slv12,Slv13,Slv14,Slv15 MPI_cosine
#####################################################

*** Number of processes: 16
*** processing capacity: 19.2 GHz.


Master node name: Mst0

Enter angle(deg.):

270


    270.0 deg. = -1.571 rads
Cosine(-1.571) = -0.000

real  0m8.228s
user  0m1.200s
sys   0m0.360s




alpha@Mst0:/beta/gamma $ time mpiexec -H
Mst0,Slv1,Slv2,Slv3,Slv4,Slv5,Slv6,Slv7,Slv8,
Slv9,Slv10,Slv11,Slv12,Slv13,Slv14,Slv15 MPI_cosine
#####################################################
```

```
*** Number of processes: 16
*** processing capacity: 19.2 GHz.


Master node name: Mst0

Enter angle(deg.):

300


    300.0 deg. = -1.047 rads
Cosine(-1.047) = 0.500

real  0m7.509s
user  0m1.270s
sys   0m0.350s



alpha@Mst0:/beta/gamma $ time mpiexec -H
Mst0,Slv1,Slv2,Slv3,Slv4,Slv5,Slv6,Slv7,Slv8,
Slv9,Slv10,Slv11,Slv12,Slv13,Slv14,Slv15 MPI_cosine
#######################################################

*** Number of processes: 16
*** processing capacity: 19.2 GHz.


Master node name: Mst0

Enter angle(deg.):

330


    330.0 deg. = -0.524 rads
Cosine(-0.524) = 0.866

real  0m7.167s
user  0m1.180s
sys   0m0.350s
```

```
alpha@Mst0:/beta/gamma $ time mpiexec -H
Mst0,Slv1,Slv2,Slv3,Slv4,Slv5,Slv6,Slv7,Slv8,
Slv9,Slv10,Slv11,Slv12,Slv13,Slv14,Slv15 MPI_cosine
####################################################

*** Number of processes: 16
*** processing capacity: 19.2 GHz.


Master node name: Mst0

Enter angle(deg.):

360


    360.0 deg. = -0.000 rads
Cosine(-0.000) = 1.000

real 0m10.469s
user 0m1.250s
sys  0m0.300s
```

The following figure is a plot of the MPI cosine(x) run:

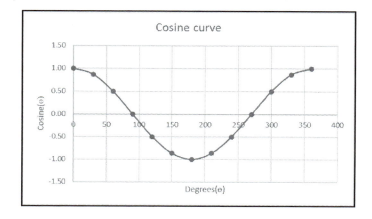

MPI Taylor series tan(x) function

Since *tan(x) = sine(x)/cosine(x)*, we could combine the Taylor series formula of the `sine(x)` and `cos(x)` to construct the tangent function as follows:

$$\tan(x) \;=\; \frac{\sum_{k=0}^{\infty}(-1^k)\times\frac{x^{2k+1}}{(2k+1)!}}{\sum_{k=0}^{\infty}(-1^k)\times\frac{x^{2k}}{(2k)!}}$$

Write, compile, and run this `Serial tangent(x)` code (see the following serial tangent(x) code) to get a feel of the program:

```
/********************************
 * Serial tangent(x) code.        *
 *                                *
 * Taylor series representation   *
 * of the trigonometric tan(x).   *
 *                                *
 * Author: Carlos R. Morrison     *
 *                                *
 * Date: 1/10/2017                *
 ********************************/
#include <math.h>
#include <stdio.h>

int main(void)
{
/***********************************************/
    unsigned int i,j,l;
    unsigned long int k;
    long long int B,D,G,I;
    int num_loops = 17;
    float y;
    double x;
    double sum=0,sum01=0,sum02=0;
    double A,C,E,F,H,J;
/***********************************************/

/***********************************************/
    printf("\n");
Z:printf("Enter angle(deg.):\n");
    printf("\n");
    scanf("%f",&y);
    if(y >= 0 && y < 90.0)
    {
```

```
    x = y*(M_PI/180.0);
  }
  else
  if(y > 90.0 && y <= 180.0)
  {
     x = -(180.0-y)*(M_PI/180.0);
  }
  else
  if(y >= 180.0 && y < 270)
  {
     x = -(180-y)*(M_PI/180.0);
  }
  else
  if(y > 270.0 && y <= 360)
  {
     x = -(360.0-y)*(M_PI/180.0);
  }
  else
  {
    printf("\n");
    printf("Bad input!! Please try another angel\n");
    printf("\n");
    goto Z;
  }
/*****************************************************
 *               ***** SINE BLOCK *****             *
 ****************************************************/
  sum01 = 0;
  for(i = 0; i < num_loops; i++)
  {
    A = (double)pow(-1,i);
    B = 2*i+1;
    C = (double)pow(x,B);

    D = 1;
    for(j = 1; j <= B; j++)
    {
      D *= j;
    }

    E = (A*C)/(double)D;

    sum01 += E;
  }// End of for(i = 0; i < num_loops; i++)

/*****************************************************
 *              ***** COSINE BLOCK *****             *
 ****************************************************/
```

```
  sum02 = 0;
  for(k = 0;  k < num_loops;  k++)
  {
    F = (double)pow(-1,k);
    G = 2*k;
    H = (double)pow(x,G);

    I = 1;
    for(l = 1;  l <= G;  l++)
    {
      I *= l;
    }

    J = (F*H)/(double)I;

    sum02 += J;
  }// End of for(k = 0; k < num_loops; k++)

/*********************************************************
 *              ***** TANGENT BLOCK *****                *
 ********************************************************/

/*******************/
  sum = sum01/sum02;  // Tan(x) ==> Sine(x)/Cos(x)
/*******************/

/********************************************************/
  printf("\n");
  printf("%.1f deg. = %.3f rads\n", y, x);
  printf("Tan(%.1f) = %.3f\n", y, sum);

  return 0;
}
```

Next, write, compile, and run the MPI version of the preceding serial
tan(x) code (see MPI tan(x) code below), using one processor from each of
the 16 nodes.

```
/********************************
 * MPI tangent(x) code.         *
 *                              *
 * Taylor series representation *
 * of the trigonometric tan(x). *
 *                              *
 * Author: Carlos R. Morrison   *
 *                              *
 * Date: 1/10/2017              *
 ********************************/
#include <mpi.h>  // (Open)MPI library
```

```c
#include <math.h> // math library
#include <stdio.h>// Standard Input/Output library

int main(int argc, char*argv[])
{
/************************************************************************
****/
  unsigned int i,j,l;
  unsigned long int k,m,n;
  long long int B,D,G,I;
  int Q = 17,rank,length,numprocs;
  float x,y;
  double sum,sum1,sum2,sum01=0,sum02=0,rank_sum,rank_sum1,rank_sum2;
  double A,C,E,F,H,J;
  char hostname[MPI_MAX_PROCESSOR_NAME];

  MPI_Init(&argc, &argv);                      // initiates MPI
  MPI_Comm_size(MPI_COMM_WORLD, &numprocs);   // acquire number of processes
  MPI_Comm_rank(MPI_COMM_WORLD, &rank);       // acquire current process id
  MPI_Get_processor_name(hostname, &length); // acquire hostname
/************************************************************************
****/

  if(rank == 0)
  {
    printf("\n");
    printf("############################################################");
    printf("\n\n");
    printf("*** Number of processes: %d\n",numprocs);
    printf("*** processing capacity: %.1f GHz.\n",numprocs*1.2);
    printf("\n\n");
    printf("Master node name: %s\n", hostname);
    printf("\n");
    printf("\n");
 Z: printf("Enter angle(deg.):\n");
    printf("\n");
    scanf("%f",&y);

    if(y >= 0 && y < 90.0)
    {
      x = y*(M_PI/180.0);
    }
    else
    if(y > 90.0 && y <= 180.0)
    {
      x = -(180.0-y)*(M_PI/180.0);
    }
    else
```

```
    if(y >= 180.0 && y < 270)
    {
      x = -(180-y)*(M_PI/180.0);
    }
    else
    if(y > 270.0 && y <= 360)
    {
      x = -(360.0-y)*(M_PI/180.0);
    }
    else
    {
      printf("\n");
      printf("Bad input!! Please try another angel\n");
      printf("\n");
      goto Z;
    }
  }// End of if(rank == 0)
/**************************************************************************
****/

//broadcast to all processes, the number of segments you want
  MPI_Bcast(&Q, 1, MPI_INT, 0, MPI_COMM_WORLD);
  MPI_Bcast(&x, 1, MPI_INT, 0, MPI_COMM_WORLD);
// this loop increments the maximum number of iterations, thus providing
// additional work for testing computational speed of the processors

//for(total_iter = 1; total_iter < Q; total_iter++)
  {
    sum01 = 0;
    sum02 = 0;
//   for(total_iter = 1; i < total_iter; total_iter++)
    for(i = rank + 1; i <= Q; i += numprocs)
    {
      m = (i-1);
     /****************************************************
      *                 ***** SINE BLOCK *****          *
      ****************************************************/
      A = (double)pow(-1,m);
      B = 2*m+1;
      C = (double)pow(x,B);

      D = 1;
      for(j = 1; j <= B; j++)
      {
        D *= j;
      }

      E = (A*C)/(double)D;
```

```
    sum01 += E;


    /*****************************************************
     *               ***** COSINE BLOCK *****            *
     *****************************************************/
    F = (double)pow(-1,m);
    G = 2*m;
    H = (double)pow(x,G);

    I = 1;
    for(l = 1; l <= G; l++)
    {
      I *= l;
    }

    J = (F*H)/(double)I;

    sum02 += J;
  }// End of for(i = rank + 1; i <= Q; i += numprocs)

  rank_sum1 = sum01;
  rank_sum2 = sum02;

//collect and add the partial sum0 values from all processes
    MPI_Reduce(&rank_sum1, &sum1, 1, MPI_DOUBLE,MPI_SUM, 0,
MPI_COMM_WORLD);
    MPI_Reduce(&rank_sum2, &sum2, 1, MPI_DOUBLE,MPI_SUM, 0,
MPI_COMM_WORLD);
  }//End of for(total_iter = 1; total_iter < n; total_iter++)

  if(rank == 0)
  {
    sum = sum1/sum2;// Tan(x) ==> Sine(x)/Cos(x)
    printf("\n");
    printf("%.1f deg. = %.3f rads\n", y, x);
    printf("Tan(%.1f) = %.3f\n", y, sum);
  }

// clean up, done with MPI
  MPI_Finalize();

  return 0;
}// End of int main(int argc, char*argv[])
```

Now, we will check the MPI `tan(x)` **run:**

```
alpha@Mst0:/beta/gamma $ time mpiexec -H
Mst0,Slv1,Slv2,Slv3,Slv4,Slv5,Slv6,Slv7,Slv8,
Slv9,Slv10,Slv11,Slv12,Slv13,Slv14,Slv15 MPI_tan
######################################################

*** Number of processes: 16
*** processing capacity: 19.2 GHz.
Master node name: Mst0


Enter angle(deg.):

0

0.0 deg. = 0.000 rads
Tan(0.0) = 0.000

real 0m19.636s
user 0m1.180s
sys  0m0.430s



alpha@Mst0:/beta/gamma $ time mpiexec -H
Mst0,Slv1,Slv2,Slv3,Slv4,Slv5,Slv6,Slv7,Slv8,
Slv9,Slv10,Slv11,Slv12,Slv13,Slv14,Slv15 MPI_tan
######################################################

*** Number of processes: 16
*** processing capacity: 19.2 GHz.


Master node name: Mst0


Enter angle(deg.):

30

30.0 deg. = 0.524 rads
Tan(30.0) = 0.577

real 0m13.139s
user 0m1.360s
sys  0m0.260s
```

```
alpha@Mst0:/beta/gamma $ time mpiexec -H
Mst0,Slv1,Slv2,Slv3,Slv4,Slv5,Slv6,Slv7,Slv8,
Slv9,Slv10,Slv11,Slv12,Slv13,Slv14,Slv15 MPI_tan
#####################################################

*** Number of processes: 16
*** processing capacity: 19.2 GHz.


Master node name: Mst0


Enter angle(deg.):
60

60.0 deg. = 1.047 rads
Tan(60.0) = 1.732

real 0m7.451s
user 0m1.250s
sys  0m0.330s



alpha@Mst0:/beta/gamma $ time mpiexec -H
Mst0,Slv1,Slv2,Slv3,Slv4,Slv5,Slv6,Slv7,Slv8,
Slv9,Slv10,Slv11,Slv12,Slv13,Slv14,Slv15 MPI_tan
#####################################################

*** Number of processes: 16
*** processing capacity: 19.2 GHz.


Master node name: Mst0


Enter angle(deg.):

90

Bad input!! Please try another angel

Enter angle(deg.):

120

120.0 deg. = -1.047 rads
Tan(120.0) = -1.732
```

```
real  0m17.420s
user  0m1.210s
sys   0m0.360s



alpha@Mst0:/beta/gamma $ time mpiexec -H
Mst0,Slv1,Slv2,Slv3,Slv4,Slv5,Slv6,Slv7,Slv8,
Slv9,Slv10,Slv11,Slv12,Slv13,Slv14,Slv15 MPI_tan
########################################################

*** Number of processes: 16
*** processing capacity: 19.2 GHz.


Master node name: Mst0

Enter angle(deg.):
150

150.0 deg. = -0.524 rads
Tan(150.0) = -0.577

real  0m11.704s
user  0m1.410s
sys   0m0.370s



alpha@Mst0:/beta/gamma $ time mpiexec -H
Mst0,Slv1,Slv2,Slv3,Slv4,Slv5,Slv6,Slv7,Slv8,
Slv9,Slv10,Slv11,Slv12,Slv13,Slv14,Slv15 MPI_tan
########################################################

*** Number of processes: 16
*** processing capacity: 19.2 GHz.


Master node name: Mst0


Enter angle(deg.):

180

180.0 deg. = -0.000 rads
Tan(180.0) = 0.000
```

```
real  0m5.871s
user  0m1.190s
sys   0m0.370s



alpha@Mst0:/beta/gamma $ time mpiexec -H
Mst0,Slv1,Slv2,Slv3,Slv4,Slv5,Slv6,Slv7,Slv8,
Slv9,Slv10,Slv11,Slv12,Slv13,Slv14,Slv15 MPI_tan
#########################################################

*** Number of processes: 16
*** processing capacity: 19.2 GHz.


Master node name: Mst0


Enter angle(deg.):

210

210.0 deg. = 0.524 rads
Tan(210.0) = 0.577
real  1m8.558s
user  0m1.190s
sys   0m0.550s



alpha@Mst0:/beta/gamma $ time mpiexec -H
Mst0,Slv1,Slv2,Slv3,Slv4,Slv5,Slv6,Slv7,Slv8,
Slv9,Slv10,Slv11,Slv12,Slv13,Slv14,Slv15 MPI_tan
#########################################################

*** Number of processes: 16
*** processing capacity: 19.2 GHz.


Master node name: Mst0


Enter angle(deg.):

240

240.0 deg. = 1.047 rads
Tan(240.0) = 1.732
```

```
real  0m22.489s
user  0m1.310s
sys   0m0.270s


alpha@Mst0:/beta/gamma $ time mpiexec -H
Mst0,Slv1,Slv2,Slv3,Slv4,Slv5,Slv6,Slv7,Slv8,
Slv9,Slv10,Slv11,Slv12,Slv13,Slv14,Slv15 MPI_tan
#########################################################

*** Number of processes: 16
*** processing capacity: 19.2 GHz.


Master node name: Mst0


Enter angle(deg.):

270

Bad input!! Please try another angel

Enter angle(deg.):

300

300.0 deg. = -1.047 rads
Tan(300.0) = -1.732

real  0m15.178s
user  0m1.180s
sys   0m0.410s


alpha@Mst0:/beta/gamma $ time mpiexec -H
Mst0,Slv1,Slv2,Slv3,Slv4,Slv5,Slv6,Slv7,Slv8,
Slv9,Slv10,Slv11,Slv12,Slv13,Slv14,Slv15 MPI_tan
#########################################################

*** Number of processes: 16
*** processing capacity: 19.2 GHz.


Master node name: Mst0
```

```
Enter angle(deg.):

330

330.0 deg. = -0.524 rads
Tan(330.0) = -0.577

real  0m7.067s
user  0m1.200s
sys   0m0.370s




alpha@Mst0:/beta/gamma $ time mpiexec -H
Mst0,Slv1,Slv2,Slv3,Slv4,Slv5,Slv6,Slv7,Slv8,
Slv9,Slv10,Slv11,Slv12,Slv13,Slv14,Slv15 MPI_tan
#######################################################

*** Number of processes: 16
*** processing capacity: 19.2 GHz.


Master node name: Mst0


Enter angle(deg.):

360

360.0 deg. = -0.000 rads
Tan(360.0) = 0.000

real  0m6.489s
user  0m1.200s
sys   0m0.340s
```

The following figure is a plot of the MPI `tan(x)` run:

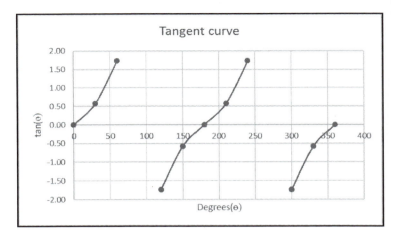

MPI Taylor series ln(x) function

The Taylor series formula for the `ln(x)` function is as follows:

$$\ln(x) = 2 \sum_{k=0}^{\infty} \frac{1}{(2k-1)} \times \left(\frac{x-1}{x+1}\right)^{2k-1}$$

Write, compile, and run this `Serial ln(x)` code (see the following screenshot, which shows `Serial ln(x)` code) to get a feel of the program:

```
/*********************************
 * Serial ln(x) code.            *
 *                               *
 * Taylor series representation  *
 * of the trigonometric ln(x).   *
 *                               *
 * Author: Carlos R. Morrison    *
 *                               *
 * Date: 1/10/2017               *
 *********************************/
#include <math.h>
#include <stdio.h>
int main(void)
{
```

```
  Unsigned int n;
  Unsigned long int k;
  double A,B,C;
  double sum=0;
  long int num_loops;
  float x,y;
/*********************************************************/
  printf("\n");
  printf("\n");
  printf("Enter the number of iterations:\n");
  printf("\n");
  scanf("%d",&n);
  printf("\n");
Z:printf("Enter x value:\n");
  printf("\n");
  scanf("%f",&y);

  if(y > 0.0)
  {
    x = y;
  }
  else
  {
    printf("\n");
    printf("Bad input!! Please try another value\n");
    printf("\n");
    goto Z;
  }
/*********************************************************/
  sum = 0;
  for(k = 1;  k < n;  k++)
  {
    A = 1.0/(double)(2*k-1);
    B = pow(((x-1)/(x+1)),(2*k-1));
    C = A*B;

    sum += C;
  }
  printf("\n");
  printf("ln(%.1f) = %.16f\n", y, 2.0*sum);
  printf("\n");

  return 0;
}
```

Next, write, compile, and run the MPI version of the preceding serial ln(x) code (see MPI ln(x) code below), using one processor from each of the 16 nodes.

```
/*********************************
 * MPI ln(x) code.              *
 *                              *
 * Taylor series representation *
 * of the trigonometric ln(x).  *
 *                              *
 * Author: Carlos R. Morrison   *
 *                              *
 * Date: 1/10/2017              *
 *********************************/

#include <mpi.h>
#include <math.h>
#include <stdio.h>

int main(int argc, char*argv[])
{
/**********************************************************/
  long long int total_iter;
  Unsigned int n;
  Unsigned long int k;
  int rank,length,numprocs,i;
  float x,y;
  double sum,sum0,A,C,B,rank_sum;
  char hostname[MPI_MAX_PROCESSOR_NAME];

  MPI_Init(&argc, &argv);                      // initiates MPI
  MPI_Comm_size(MPI_COMM_WORLD, &numprocs);    // acquire number of processes
  MPI_Comm_rank(MPI_COMM_WORLD, &rank);        // acquire current process id
  MPI_Get_processor_name(hostname, &length);   // acquire hostname
/**********************************************************/

  if(rank == 0)
  {
    printf("\n");
    printf("#########################################################");
    printf("\n\n");
    printf("*** Number of processes: %d\n",numprocs);
    printf("*** processing capacity: %.1f GHz.\n",numprocs*1.2);
    printf("\n\n");
    printf("Master node name: %s\n", hostname);
    printf("\n");
    printf("\n");
    printf("Enter the number of iterations:\n");
    printf("\n");
    scanf("%d",&n);
    printf("\n");
  Z:printf("Enter x value:\n");
```

```c
      printf("\n");
      scanf("%f",&y);

      if(y > 0.0)
      {
        x = y;
      }
      else
      {
        printf("\n");
        printf("Bad input!! Please try another value\n");
        printf("\n");
        goto Z;
      }
   }// End of if(rank == 0)

// broadcast to all processes, the number of segments you want
   MPI_Bcast(&n, 1, MPI_INT, 0, MPI_COMM_WORLD);
   MPI_Bcast(&x, 1, MPI_INT, 0, MPI_COMM_WORLD);

//this loop increments the maximum number of iterations, thus providing
//additional work for testing computational speed of the processors
//for(total_iter = 1; total_iter < n; total_iter++)
   {
      sum0 = 0.0;
//   for(i = rank + 1; i <= total_iter; i += numprocs)
      for(i = rank + 1; i <= n; i += numprocs)
      {
        k = i;

        A = 1.0/(double)(2*k-1);
        B = pow(((x-1)/(x+1)),(2*k-1));
        C = A*B;

        sum0 += C;
      }

      rank_sum = sum0;// Partial sum for a given rank

//   collect and add the partial sum0 values from all processes
      MPI_Reduce(&rank_sum, &sum, 1, MPI_DOUBLE,MPI_SUM, 0, MPI_COMM_WORLD);
   }// End of for(total_iter = 1; total_iter < n; total_iter++)

   if(rank == 0)
   {
     printf("\n");
     printf("ln(%.1f) = %.16f\n", y, 2.0*sum);
     printf("\n");
```

```
    }


//clean up, done with MPI
    MPI_Finalize();

    return 0;
}// End of int main(int argc, char*argv[])
```

Let's look at the MPI ln(x) run:

```
alpha@Mst0:/beta/gamma $ time mpiexec -H
Mst0,Slv1,Slv2,Slv3,Slv4,Slv5,Slv6,Slv7,Slv8,
Slv9,Slv10,Slv11,Slv12,Slv13,Slv14,Slv15 MPI_ln
####################################################

*** Number of processes: 16
*** processing capacity: 19.2 GHz.

Master node name: Mst0

Enter the number of iterations:

500000

Enter x value:

0.5

ln(0.5) = -0.6931472029116872

real 0m16.654s
user 0m1.300s
sys  0m0.300s



alpha@Mst0:/beta/gamma $ time mpiexec -H
Mst0,Slv1,Slv2,Slv3,Slv4,Slv5,Slv6,Slv7,Slv8,
Slv9,Slv10,Slv11,Slv12,Slv13,Slv14,Slv15 MPI_ln
####################################################

*** Number of processes: 16
*** processing capacity: 19.2 GHz.

Master node name: Mst0
```

```
Enter the number of iterations:

500000

Enter x value:

1.0

ln(1.0) = 0.0000000000000000

real  0m12.230s
user  0m1.220s
sys   0m0.370s



alpha@Mst0:/beta/gamma $ time mpiexec -H
Mst0,Slv1,Slv2,Slv3,Slv4,Slv5,Slv6,Slv7,Slv8,
Slv9,Slv10,Slv11,Slv12,Slv13,Slv14,Slv15 MPI_ln
########################################################

*** Number of processes: 16
*** processing capacity: 19.2 GHz.

Master node name: Mst0

Enter the number of iterations:

500000

Enter x value:

3

ln(3.0) = 1.0986122886681096

real  0m14.623s
user  0m1.350s
sys   0m0.230s



alpha@Mst0:/beta/gamma $ time mpiexec -H
Mst0,Slv1,Slv2,Slv3,Slv4,Slv5,Slv6,Slv7,Slv8,
Slv9,Slv10,Slv11,Slv12,Slv13,Slv14,Slv15 MPI_ln
########################################################

*** Number of processes: 16
```

```
*** processing capacity: 19.2 GHz.

Master node name: Mst0

Enter the number of iterations:

500000

Enter x value:

5

ln(5.0) = 1.6094379839596757

real 0m15.789s
user 0m1.350s
sys  0m0.310s



alpha@Mst0:/beta/gamma $ time mpiexec -H
Mst0,Slv1,Slv2,Slv3,Slv4,Slv5,Slv6,Slv7,Slv8,
Slv9,Slv10,Slv11,Slv12,Slv13,Slv14,Slv15 MPI_ln
#######################################################

*** Number of processes: 16
*** processing capacity: 19.2 GHz.

Master node name: Mst0

Enter the number of iterations:

500000

Enter x value:

7

ln(7.0) = 1.9459101490553135

real 0m13.423s
user 0m1.450s
sys  0m0.370s



alpha@Mst0:/beta/gamma $ time mpiexec -H
Mst0,Slv1,Slv2,Slv3,Slv4,Slv5,Slv6,Slv7,Slv8,
```

```
Slv9,Slv10,Slv11,Slv12,Slv13,Slv14,Slv15 MPI_ln
#######################################################

*** Number of processes: 16
*** processing capacity: 19.2 GHz.

Master node name: Mst0

Enter the number of iterations:

500000

Enter x value:

10

ln(10.0) = 2.3025850602114915

real 0m13.351s
user 0m1.300s
sys  0m0.420s




alpha@Mst0:/beta/gamma $ time mpiexec -H
Mst0,Slv1,Slv2,Slv3,Slv4,Slv5,Slv6,Slv7,Slv8,
Slv9,Slv10,Slv11,Slv12,Slv13,Slv14,Slv15 MPI_ln
#######################################################

*** Number of processes: 16
*** processing capacity: 19.2 GHz.

Master node name: Mst0

Enter the number of iterations:

500000

Enter x value:

15

ln(15.0) = 2.7080502011022105

real 0m15.841s
user 0m1.280s
sys  0m0.410s
```

```
alpha@Mst0:/beta/gamma $ time mpiexec -H
Mst0,Slv1,Slv2,Slv3,Slv4,Slv5,Slv6,Slv7,Slv8,Slv9,
Slv10,Slv11,Slv12,Slv13,Slv14,Slv15 MPI_ln
######################################################

*** Number of processes: 16
*** processing capacity: 19.2 GHz.

Master node name: Mst0

Enter the number of iterations:

500000

Enter x value:

20

ln(20.0) = 2.9957323361388699

real  0m15.444s
user  0m1.250s
sys   0m0.370s


alpha@Mst0:/beta/gamma $ time mpiexec -H
Mst0,Slv1,Slv2,Slv3,Slv4,Slv5,Slv6,Slv7,Slv8,
Slv9,Slv10,Slv11,Slv12,Slv13,Slv14,Slv15 MPI_ln
######################################################

*** Number of processes: 16
*** processing capacity: 19.2 GHz.

Master node name: Mst0

Enter the number of iterations:

500000

Enter x value:

25

ln(25.0) = 3.2188758868570337

real  0m18.145s
user  0m1.330s
```

```
sys    0m0.280s


alpha@Mst0:/beta/gamma $ time mpiexec -H
Mst0,Slv1,Slv2,Slv3,Slv4,Slv5,Slv6,Slv7,Slv8,
Slv9,Slv10,Slv11,Slv12,Slv13,Slv14,Slv15 MPI_ln
####################################################

*** Number of processes: 16
*** processing capacity: 19.2 GHz.

Master node name: Mst0

Enter the number of iterations:

500000

Enter x value:

30

ln(30.0) = 3.4011974124578881

real 0m15.000s
user 0m1.270s
sys    0m0.360s
```

The following figure is a plot of the MPI $\ln(x)$ run:

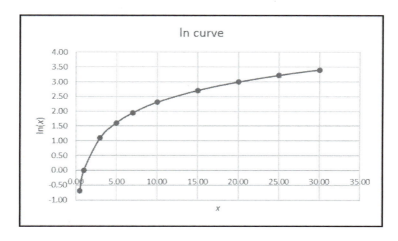

Summary

In this chapter, we learned how to write and run the serial and MPI versions of the Taylor series expansion for the sine function, the cosine function, the tangent function, and the natural log (`ln`) function.

10
Real-World Physics Application

We will now investigate the concurrent (MPI) wave code for a vibrating string. It is a point-to-point communication example that should give your Pi a good workout.

In this chapter, you will learn:

- How to write and run the MPI code for a vibrating string

MPI concurrent wave equation and code

The following code was borrowed from Blaise Barney of Lawrence Livermore National Laboratory. It is an MPI concurrent wave equation program that the author implemented on his 64-core Pi3 supercomputer.

The code essentially solves a one-dimensional wave equation and it has the following form:

$$A(i,t+1) = (2.0*A(i,t)) - A(i,t-1)+(c*(A(i-1,t)-(2.0*A(i,t))+A(i+1,t)))$$

Please see; http://www.robopgmr.com/?p=2780 for more in-depth details and instructions.

Additionally, the code discretizes said vibrating string into points (100 in this slightly modified version of the code) along its length, and calculates the amplitudes of those points as per the number of time steps values (five for this code run) you entered initially, and then displays the results. The author employed all 64 cores of his Pi3 to generate the amplitudes at the points.

The code was initially executed/tested on the author's main PC. The .c file was subsequently SFTP over to the master node on his Pi3 super cluster, where it was then compiled in the export gamma folder. The code file provided with this book has the name BK_wave4.c.

On the master node, write, compile, and run the concurrent wave code depicted here:

```
/*****************************************************************
**
 * FILE: mpi_wave.c
 *
 * OTHER FILES: draw_wave.c
 *
 * DESCRIPTION:
 *
 *   MPI Concurrent Wave Equation - C Version
 *
 *   Point-to-Point Communications Example
 *
 *   This program implements the concurrent wave equation described
 *
 *   in Chapter 5 of Fox et al., 1988, Solving Problems on Concurrent
 *
 *   Processors, vol 1.
 *
 *   A vibrating string is decomposed into points. Each processor is
 *
 *   responsible for updating the amplitude of a number of points over
 *
 *   time. At each iteration, each processor exchanges boundary points with
 *
 *   nearest neighbors. This version uses low level sends and receives
 *
 *   to exchange boundary points.
 *
 *  AUTHOR: Blaise Barney. Adapted from Ros Leibensperger, Cornell Theory
 *
 *    Center. Converted to MPI: George L. Gusciora, MHPCC (1/95)
 *
 * LAST REVISED: 07/05/05
 *
 *****************************************************************
**/
#include "mpi.h"
#include <stdio.h>
#include <stdlib.h>
#include <math.h>
```

```
#define MASTER 0
#define TPOINTS 100//800 ç The author made this modification.
#define MAXSTEPS   10000
#define PI 3.14159265

int RtoL = 10;
int LtoR = 20;
int OUT1 = 30;
int OUT2 = 40;

void init_master(void);
void init_workers(void);
void init_line(void);
void update (int left, int right);
void output_master(void);
void output_workers(void);
externvoid draw_wave(double *);

int       taskid,                /* task ID */
    numtasks,              /* number of processes */
    nsteps,                /* number of time steps */
    npoints,               /* number of points handled by this processor */
    first;                 /* index of 1st point handled by this processor */
double etime,              /* elapsed time in seconds */
    values[TPOINTS+2],     /* values at time t */
    oldval[TPOINTS+2],     /* values at time (t-dt) */
    newval[TPOINTS+2];     /* values at time (t+dt) */

/*  -------------------------------------------------------------------
 *   Master obtains time step input value from user and broadcasts it
 *  ------------------------------------------------------------------- */
void init_master(void)
{
  char tchar[8];
/* Set number of number of time steps and then print and broadcast*/
  nsteps = 0;
  while ((nsteps < 1) || (nsteps > MAXSTEPS))
  {
    printf("\n");
    printf("Enter number of time steps (1-%d): \n",MAXSTEPS);
    scanf("%s", tchar);
    nsteps = atoi(tchar);
    if((nsteps < 1) || (nsteps > MAXSTEPS))
    {
      printf("Enter value between 1 and %d\n", MAXSTEPS);
    }
  }
  MPI_Bcast(&nsteps, 1, MPI_INT, MASTER, MPI_COMM_WORLD);
```

```
}// End of void init_master(void)

/*    ----------------------------------------------------------------
 *    Workers receive time step input value from master
 *    ---------------------------------------------------------------*/
void init_workers(void)
{
    MPI_Bcast(&nsteps, 1, MPI_INT, MASTER, MPI_COMM_WORLD);
  }

/*    ----------------------------------------------------------------
 *    All processes initialize points on line
 *    --------------------------------------------------------------- */
 void init_line(void)
 {
   int nmin, nleft, npts, i, j, k;
   double x, fac;

/* calculate initial values based on sine curve */
   nmin = TPOINTS/numtasks;
   nleft = TPOINTS % numtasks;
   fac = 2.0 * PI;
   for(i = 0, k = 0; i < numtasks; i++)
   {
     npts = (i < nleft) ? nmin + 1 : nmin;
     if(taskid == i)
     {
       first = k + 1;
       npoints = npts;
       printf("task=%3d first point=%5d npoints=%4d\n", taskid, first,
                                                          npts);

       for(j = 1; j <= npts; j++, k++)
       {
         x = (double)k/(double)(TPOINTS - 1);
         values[j] = sin (fac * x);
       }
     }
     else k += npts;
   }
   for(i = 1; i <= npoints; i++)
   {
     oldval[i] = values[i];
   }
 }//End of void init_line(void)


/*    ----------------------------------------------------------------
 *    All processes update their points a specified number of times
```

```
 *    ------------------------------------------------------------*/
void update(int left, int right)
{
  int i,j;
  double dtime, c, dx, tau, sqtau;
  MPI_Status status;

  dtime = 0.3;
  c = 1.0;
  dx = 1.0;
  tau = (c * dtime / dx);
  sqtau = tau * tau;

/* Update values for each point along string */
  for(i = 1; i <= nsteps; i++)
  {
/* Exchange data with "left-hand" neighbor */
  if(first != 1)
  {
     MPI_Send(&values[1], 1, MPI_DOUBLE, left, RtoL, MPI_COMM_WORLD);
     MPI_Recv(&values[0], 1, MPI_DOUBLE, left, LtoR, MPI_COMM_WORLD,
     &status);
  }
/* Exchange data with "right-hand" neighbor */
  if(first + npoints -1 != TPOINTS)
  {
     MPI_Send(&values[npoints], 1, MPI_DOUBLE, right, LtoR,
     MPI_COMM_WORLD);
     MPI_Recv(&values[npoints+1], 1, MPI_DOUBLE, right, RtoL,
     MPI_COMM_WORLD, &status);
  }
/* Update points along line */
  for(j = 1; j <= npoints; j++)
  {
/* Global endpoints */
     if((first + j - 1 == 1) || (first + j - 1 == TPOINTS))
     newval[j] = 0.0;
        else
/* Use wave equation to update points */
        newval[j] = (2.0 * values[j]) - oldval[j]
           + (sqtau * (values[j-1] - (2.0 * values[j]) + values[j+1]));
     }// End of for(j = 1; j <= npoints; j++)
     for(j = 1; j <= npoints; j++)
     {
       oldval[j] = values[j];
       values[j] = newval[j];
     }
   }// End of for (i = 1; i <= nsteps; i++)
```

```
  }// End of void update(int left, int right)

  /*  --------------------------------------------------------------
   *  Master receives results from workers and prints
   *  -------------------------------------------------------------- */
  void output_master(void)
  {
    int i, j, source, start, npts, buffer[2];
    double results[TPOINTS];
    MPI_Status status;

  /* Store worker's results in results array */
    for(i = 1; i < numtasks; i++)
    {
  /* Receive first point, number of points and results */
        MPI_Recv(buffer, 2, MPI_INT, i, OUT1, MPI_COMM_WORLD, &status);
        start = buffer[0];
        npts = buffer[1];
        MPI_Recv(&results[start-1], npts, MPI_DOUBLE, i, OUT2,
        MPI_COMM_WORLD, &status);
    }
  /* Store master's results in results array */
    for(i = first; i < first + npoints; i++)
    {
      results[i-1] = values[i];
    }
    j = 0;
  printf("***************************************************************\n");
  printf("Final amplitude values for all points after %d steps:\n", nsteps);
  for(i = 0; i < TPOINTS; i++)
  {
      printf("%6.2f ", results[i]);
      j = j++;
      if(j == 10)
      {
        printf("\n");
        j = 0;
      }
  }
  printf("***************************************************************\n");
  printf("\nDrawing graph...\n");
  printf("Click the EXIT button or use CTRL-C to quit\n");

  /* display results with draw_wave routine */
  //  draw_wave(&results[0]); //                     <===================>
  }// End of void output_master(void)

  /*  --------------------------------------------------------------
```

```
 *    Workers send the updated values to the master
 *    ----------------------------------------------------------------*/

void output_workers(void)
{
    int buffer[2];
    MPI_Status status;

/* Send first point, number of points and results to master */
    buffer[0] = first;
    buffer[1] = npoints;
    MPI_Send(&buffer, 2, MPI_INT, MASTER, OUT1, MPI_COMM_WORLD);
    MPI_Send(&values[1], npoints, MPI_DOUBLE, MASTER, OUT2,
    MPI_COMM_WORLD);
}// End of void output_workers(void)


/*    ---------------------------------------------------------------
 *    Main program
 *    --------------------------------------------------------------- */

int main (int argc, char *argv[])
{
    int left, right, rc;
/* Initialize MPI */
    MPI_Init(&argc,&argv);
    MPI_Comm_rank(MPI_COMM_WORLD,&taskid);
    MPI_Comm_size(MPI_COMM_WORLD,&numtasks);
    if(numtasks < 2)
    {
        printf("ERROR: Number of MPI tasks set to %d\n",numtasks);
        printf("Need at least 2 tasks!  Quitting...\n");
        MPI_Abort(MPI_COMM_WORLD, rc);
        exit(0);
    }

/* Determine left and right neighbors */
    if(taskid == numtasks-1)
    {
        right = 0;
    }
    else
    {
        right = taskid + 1;
    }
    if(taskid == 0)
    {
        left = numtasks - 1;
```

```
  }
  else
  {
    left = taskid - 1;
  }


/* Get program parameters and initialize wave values */
  if(taskid == MASTER)
  {
    printf("\n");
    printf ("Starting mpi_wave using %d tasks.\n", numtasks);
    printf ("Using %d points on the vibrating string.\n", TPOINTS);
    init_master();
  }
  else
  {
    init_workers();
  }
  init_line();

/* Update values along the line for nstep time steps */
  update(left, right);

/* Master collects results from workers and prints */
  if(taskid == MASTER)
  {
    output_master();
  }
  else
  {
    output_workers();
  }
  MPI_Finalize();

  return 0;
}// End of int main (int argc, char *argv[])
```

Let's look at the MPI concurrent wave run:

```
alpha@Mst0:/beta/gamma $ time mpiexec -H
Mst0,Mst0,Mst0,Mst0,Slv1,Slv1,Slv1,Slv1,Slv2,Slv2,Slv2,Slv2,Slv3,Slv3,Slv3,
Slv3,Slv4,Slv4,Slv4,Slv4,Slv5,Slv5,Slv5,Slv5,Slv6,Slv6,Slv6,Slv6,Slv7,Slv7,
Slv7,Slv7,Slv8,Slv8,Slv8,Slv8,Slv9,Slv9,Slv9,Slv9,Slv10,Slv10,Slv10,Slv10,S
lv11,Slv11,Slv11,Slv11,Slv12,Slv12,Slv12,Slv12,Slv13,Slv13,Slv13,Slv13,Slv1
4,Slv14,Slv14,Slv14,Slv15,Slv15,Slv15,Slv15 BK_wave4
```

```
Starting mpi_wave using 64 tasks.

Using 100 points on the vibrating string.

Enter number of time steps (1-10000):

5

task= 3 first point= 7 npoints= 2

task= 0 first point= 1 npoints= 2

task= 1 first point= 3 npoints= 2

task= 2 first point= 5 npoints= 2

task= 9 first point= 19 npoints= 2

task= 33 first point= 67 npoints= 2

task= 53 first point= 90 npoints= 1

task= 57 first point= 94 npoints= 1

task= 29 first point= 59 npoints= 2

task= 21 first point= 43 npoints= 2

task= 37 first point= 74 npoints= 1

task= 41 first point= 78 npoints= 1

task= 13 first point= 27 npoints= 2

task= 51 first point= 88 npoints= 1

task= 5 first point= 11 npoints= 2

task= 45 first point= 82 npoints= 1

task= 25 first point= 51 npoints= 2

task= 19 first point= 39 npoints= 2

task= 11 first point= 23 npoints= 2

task= 35 first point= 71 npoints= 2
```

```
task= 38 first point= 75 npoints= 1

task= 61 first point= 98 npoints= 1

task= 43 first point= 80 npoints= 1

task= 50 first point= 87 npoints= 1

task= 18 first point= 37 npoints= 2

task= 34 first point= 69 npoints= 2

task= 40 first point= 77 npoints= 1

task= 48 first point= 85 npoints= 1

task= 6 first point= 13 npoints= 2

task= 16 first point= 33 npoints= 2

task= 8 first point= 17 npoints= 2

task= 10 first point= 21 npoints= 2

task= 32 first point= 65 npoints= 2

task= 59 first point= 96 npoints= 1

task= 36 first point= 73 npoints= 1

task= 49 first point= 86 npoints= 1

task= 4 first point= 9 npoints= 2

task= 17 first point= 35 npoints= 2

task= 27 first point= 55 npoints= 2

task= 42 first point= 79 npoints= 1

task= 24 first point= 49 npoints= 2

task= 14 first point= 29 npoints= 2

task= 46 first point= 83 npoints= 1

task= 56 first point= 93 npoints= 1
```

```
task= 26 first point= 53 npoints= 2

task= 20 first point= 41 npoints= 2

task= 58 first point= 95 npoints= 1

task= 22 first point= 45 npoints= 2

task= 39 first point= 76 npoints= 1

task= 54 first point= 91 npoints= 1

task= 7 first point= 15 npoints= 2

task= 62 first point= 99 npoints= 1

task= 30 first point= 61 npoints= 2

task= 44 first point= 81 npoints= 1

task= 52 first point= 89 npoints= 1

task= 12 first point= 25 npoints= 2

task= 15 first point= 31 npoints= 2

task= 47 first point= 84 npoints= 1

task= 23 first point= 47 npoints= 2

task= 55 first point= 92 npoints= 1

task= 28 first point= 57 npoints= 2

task= 31 first point= 63 npoints= 2

task= 63 first point= 100 npoints= 1

task= 60 first point= 97 npoints= 1
```

* *

The final amplitude values for all points after five steps are as follows:

```
0.00 0.06 0.13 0.19 0.25 0.31 0.37 0.43 0.48 0.54 0.59 0.64 0.69 0.73 0.77
0.81 0.85 0.88 0.90 0.93 0.95 0.97 0.98 0.99 0.99 0.99 0.99 0.98 0.97 0.96
0.94 0.92 0.89 0.86 0.83 0.79 0.75 0.71 0.66 0.61 0.56 0.51 0.46 0.40 0.34
0.28 0.22 0.16 0.09 0.03 -0.03 -0.09 -0.16 -0.22 -0.28 -0.34 -0.40 -0.46
-0.51 -0.56 -0.61 -0.66 -0.71 -0.75 -0.79 -0.83 -0.86 -0.89 -0.92 -0.94
-0.96 -0.97 -0.98 -0.99 -0.99 -0.99 -0.99 -0.98 -0.97 -0.95 -0.93 -0.90
-0.88 -0.85 -0.81 -0.77 -0.73 -0.69 -0.64 -0.59 -0.54 -0.48 -0.43 -0.37
-0.31 -0.25 -0.19 -0.13 -0.06 0.00
*************************************************************************
```

Drawing graphs

Click *ESC* or use *CTRL -C* to quit:

```
real 0m4.201s

user 0m4.960s

sys 0m5.090s

alpha@Mst0:/beta/gamma $
```

The following figure is a plot of the **Concurrent wave** run data:

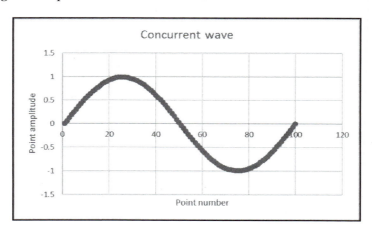

Discretized wave form

Summary

In this chapter, we learned how to write and run an MPI `concurrent  wave` function, which simulates the vibrating motion of a string.

11
Real-World Engineering Application

This chapter discusses how to generate a sawtooth signal or curve. These wave shapes are often displayed on oscilloscopes in engineering, and science labs, and in textbooks. In this chapter, you will learn:

- How to write and run the serial sawtooth Fourier series code, and same for the MPI version of said serial signal code

MPI Fourier series sawtooth signal

We will now generate such a signal by first writing, and running the serial Fourier series sawtooth code, and then apply MPI technique to the sawtooth Fourier series equation depicted here:

$$\text{sawtooth}(x) = \text{Amplitude} \times \left[\frac{1}{2} - \frac{1}{\pi} \sum_{k=1}^{\infty} \frac{1}{k} sin(k\theta) \right]$$

The serial `sawtooth(x)` code is depicted on the following pages. On the master node, write, compile, and run this serial `sawtooth(x)` code (see the following `serial sawtooth(x)` code) to get the feel of the program:

```
/************************************
 * *** Serial sawtooth(x) code *** *
 * *
 * Fourier series representation *
 * of the sawtooth(x) function. *
```

```
*  *
* Author: Carlos R. Morrison *
*  *
* Date: 2/12/2017 *
*********************************/
#include <math.h> // math library
#include <stdio.h>// Standard Input/Output library
int main(void)
{
int j;
unsigned long int i;
double sum0,sum1,A,B,C;
double D[100]={0},x[100]={0},d,dd=10.00,o,oo=10.0*(M_PI/180);
float Amp;
float g;
int m,n,p=36;
printf("n");
printf("##########################################################");
printf("nn");
printf("Enter number of iterations:n");
scanf("%d",&n);
printf("n");
x[0] = 0;
D[0] = 0;
o = 0;
d = 0;
for(j = 0; j <= p; j += 1)
{
o += oo;// rads
d += dd;// deg
x[j+1] = o;
D[j+1] = d;
}
printf("n");
printf("Enter amplitude:n");

nf("%f",&Amp);
printf("n");
printf("Enter frequency(Hz.):n");
scanf("%f",&g);
printf("n");
for(m = 0; m <= p; m++)
{
sum0 = 0.0;
for(i = 1; i <= n; i++)
{
A = 1.0/(double)i;
B = sin(i*g*x[m]);
```

```
C = A*B;
sum0 += C;// ç Summation element of the Fourier series.
}// End of for(i = 1; i <= n; i++)
sum1 = Amp*(0.5-(1.0/M_PI)*sum0);// ç Sawtooth function
printf(" x = %.3f rad, Amp. = %.3f, Deg. =
%.1fn",x[m],sum1,D[m]);
}// End of for(m = 1; m <= p; m++)
return 0;
}
```

Next, write, compile, and run the MPI version of the preceding serial sawtooth(x) code (see the following MPI sawtooth(x) code), using all 64 cores on the 16 Pi3 nodes. The MPI sawtooth(x) code, and its run are depicted on the following pages:

```
/********************************
 * of the sawtooth(x) function. *
 * *
 * Author: Carlos R. Morrison *
 * *
 * Date: 2/13/2017 *
 ********************************/
#include <mpi.h> // (Open)MPI library
#include <math.h> // math library
#include <stdio.h>// Standard Input/Output library
int main(int argc, char*argv[])
{
long long int total_iter;
int rank,length,numprocs,j;
unsigned long int i;
double sum,sum0,sum1,rank_integral,A,B,C;
double D[100]={0},sm[100]={0},d,dd=10.00,x=0.0;
float Amp,g;
int m=0,n,p=36;
char hostname[MPI_MAX_PROCESSOR_NAME];
// initiates MPI
MPI_Init(&argc, &argv);
// acquire number of processes
MPI_Comm_size(MPI_COMM_WORLD, &numprocs);
// acquire current process id
MPI_Comm_rank(MPI_COMM_WORLD, &rank);
// acquire hostname
MPI_Get_processor_name(hostname, &length);
if(rank == 0)
{
printf("n");
printf("###############################################
####");
printf("nn");
```

```
printf("*** Number of processes: %dn",numprocs);
printf("*** processing capacity: %.1f GHz.n",numprocs*1.2);
printf("nn");
printf("Master node name: %sn", hostname);
printf("n");
printf("Enter number of iterations:n");
scanf("%d",&n);
printf("n");
D[0] = 0;
d = 0;
for(j = 0; j <= p; j += 1)
{
d += dd;// deg
D[j+1] = d;
}
printf("Enter amplitude:n");
scanf("%f",&Amp);
printf("n");
printf("Enter frequency:n");
scanf("%f",&g);
printf("n");
}// End of if(rank == 0)
// broadcast g, n & x values to all processes.
Z:MPI_Bcast(&g, 1, MPI_INT, 0, MPI_COMM_WORLD);
MPI_Bcast(&n, 1, MPI_INT, 0, MPI_COMM_WORLD);
MPI_Bcast(&x, 1, MPI_INT, 0, MPI_COMM_WORLD);
// this loop increments the maximum number of iterations, thus
// providing additional work for testing computational speed of
// the processors
//for(total_iter = 1; total_iter < n; total_iter++)
{
sum0 = 0.0;
// for(i = rank + 1; i <= total_iter; i += numprocs)
for(i = rank + 1; i <= n; i += numprocs)
{
A = 1.0/(double)i;
B = sin(i*g*x);
C = A*B;
sum0 += C;// <== Summation element of the Fourier series
}// End of for(i = rank + 1; i <= n; i += numprocs)
rank_integral = sum0;// Partial sum for a given rank
// collect and add the partial sum0 values from all processes
MPI_Reduce(&rank_integral, &sum, 1, MPI_DOUBLE,MPI_SUM, 0,
MPI_COMM_WORLD);
}// End of for(total_iter = 1; total_iter < n; total_iter++)
m += 1;//counter for array angle D[]
if(rank == 0)
{
```

```
sum1 = Amp*(0.5-(1.0/M_PI)*sum);// çSawtooth function
printf("x = %.3f rad, Amp. = %.3f, Deg. = %.1fn",x,sum1,D[m-1]);
}// End of if(rank == 0)
if(m <= p)
{
x += dd*(M_PI/180);// Angle (radians) accumulator
goto Z;
}
//clean up, done with MPI
MPI_Finalize();
return 0;
}// End of int main(int argc, char*argv[])
```

The value of the individual points on the signal curve was generated using 1000 iterations (feel free to use a different iteration value to see how the quality of the generated curve changes), an amplitude of 1, and frequency 2. Feel free to change and/or improve all the codes associated with this book to see what effects ensues. The following highlighted narrative portrays the complete coding sequence, beginning with transferring the code from the main PC to the master Pi, and ultimately running the code on the Pi3 supercomputer. The narrative serves as a summary of the entire process.

Following is the narrative for MPI sawtooth(x) run:

```
carlospg@gamma:~/Desktop$ sftp pi@192.168.0.14 <= Setting up file transfer
from main PC.
pi@192.168.0.14's password: <= Enter password.
Connected to 192.168.0.14.
sftp> put 16_MPI_sawtooth.c <= Transfer file from the main PC to master Pi3
(IP address: 192.168.0.14).
Uploading 16_MPI_sawtooth.c to /home/pi/16_MPI_sawtooth.c
16_MPI_sawtooth.c 100% 3298 3.2KB/s 00:00
sftp> exit
carlospg@gamma:~/Desktop$ ssh pi@192.168.0.14 <= Logging into master Pi3
from main PC.
pi@192.168.0.14's password: <= Enter password.
The programs included with the Debian GNU/Linux system are free software;
the exact distribution terms for each program are described in the
individual files in /usr/share/doc/*/copyright.
Debian GNU/Linux comes with ABSOLUTELY NO WARRANTY, to the extent
permitted by applicable law.
Last login: Mon Feb 13 13:36:42 2017 from 192.168.0.10
pi@Mst0:~ $ su – alpha <= Change over to the "alpha" user.
Password: <= Enter password.
* keychain 2.7.1 ~ http://www.funtoo.org
* Found existing ssh-agent: 2296
* Found existing gpg-agent: 2321
* Known ssh key: /home/alpha/.ssh/id_rsa
```

```
alpha@Mst0:~ $ cd /beta/gamma <= Change directory to the code folder
(gamma).
alpha@Mst0:/beta/gamma $ cp -a /home/pi/16_MPI_sawtooth.c ./ <= Copy code
to "gamma" folder.
alpha@Mst0:/beta/gamma $ vim 16_MPI_sawtooth.c <= (optional) check if the
code is the correct version.
alpha@Mst0:/beta/gamma $ mpicc 16_MPI_sawtooth.c -o 16_MPI_sawtooth -lm <=
Compile.
alpha@Mst0:/beta/gamma $ time mpiexec -H Mst0,Mst0,Mst0,Mst0,Slv1,Slv1,
Slv1,Slv1,Slv2,Slv2,Slv2,Slv2,Slv3,Slv3,Slv3,Slv3,Slv4,Slv4,Slv4,Slv4,Slv5,
Slv5,Slv5,Slv5,Slv6,Slv6,Slv6,Slv6,Slv7,Slv7,Slv7,Slv7,Slv8,Slv8,Slv8,Slv8,
Slv9,Slv9,Slv9,Slv9,Slv10,Slv10,Slv10,Slv10,Slv11,Slv11,Slv11,Slv11,Slv12,
Slv12,Slv12,Slv12,Slv13,Slv13,Slv13,Slv13,Slv14,Slv14,Slv14,Slv14,Slv15,
Slv15,Slv15,Slv15 16_MPI_sawtooth <= Run the code using 64 cores/processes.
#########################################################
*** Number of processes: 64
*** processing capacity: 76.8 GHz.
Master node name: Mst0
Enter number of iterations:
1000
Enter amplitude:
1
Enter frequency:
2
x = 0.000 rad, Amp. = 0.500, Deg. = 0.0
x = 0.175 rad, Amp. = 0.055, Deg. = 10.0
x = 0.349 rad, Amp. = 0.111, Deg. = 20.0
x = 0.524 rad, Amp. = 0.167, Deg. = 30.0
x = 0.698 rad, Amp. = 0.222, Deg. = 40.0
x = 0.873 rad, Amp. = 0.278, Deg. = 50.0
x = 1.047 rad, Amp. = 0.333, Deg. = 60.0
x = 1.222 rad, Amp. = 0.389, Deg. = 70.0
x = 1.396 rad, Amp. = 0.444, Deg. = 80.0
x = 1.571 rad, Amp. = 0.500, Deg. = 90.0
x = 1.745 rad, Amp. = 0.556, Deg. = 100.0
x = 1.920 rad, Amp. = 0.611, Deg. = 110.0
x = 2.094 rad, Amp. = 0.667, Deg. = 120.0
x = 2.269 rad, Amp. = 0.722, Deg. = 130.0
x = 2.443 rad, Amp. = 0.778, Deg. = 140.0
x = 2.618 rad, Amp. = 0.833, Deg. = 150.0
x = 2.793 rad, Amp. = 0.889, Deg. = 160.0
x = 2.967 rad, Amp. = 0.945, Deg. = 170.0
x = 3.142 rad, Amp. = 0.500, Deg. = 180.0
x = 3.316 rad, Amp. = 0.055, Deg. = 190.0
x = 3.491 rad, Amp. = 0.111, Deg. = 200.0
x = 3.665 rad, Amp. = 0.167, Deg. = 210.0
x = 3.840 rad, Amp. = 0.222, Deg. = 220.0
x = 4.014 rad, Amp. = 0.278, Deg. = 230.0
```

```
x = 4.189 rad, Amp. = 0.333, Deg. = 240.0
x = 4.363 rad, Amp. = 0.389, Deg. = 250.0
x = 4.538 rad, Amp. = 0.444, Deg. = 260.0
x = 4.712 rad, Amp. = 0.500, Deg. = 270.0
x = 4.887 rad, Amp. = 0.556, Deg. = 280.0
x = 5.061 rad, Amp. = 0.611, Deg. = 290.0
x = 5.236 rad, Amp. = 0.667, Deg. = 300.0
x = 5.411 rad, Amp. = 0.722, Deg. = 310.0
x = 5.585 rad, Amp. = 0.778, Deg. = 320.0
x = 5.760 rad, Amp. = 0.833, Deg. = 330.0
x = 5.934 rad, Amp. = 0.889, Deg. = 340.0
x = 6.109 rad, Amp. = 0.945, Deg. = 350.0
x = 6.283 rad, Amp. = 0.500, Deg. = 360.0
real 0m8.945s
user 0m11.230s
sys 0m13.310s
alpha@Mst0:/beta/gamma $
```

The following figure is a plot of the MPI sawtooth data:

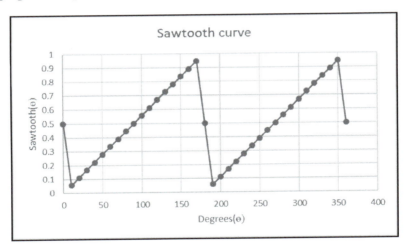

Summary

In this chapter, we learned how to write a serial sawtooth Fourier series code, and an MPI version of the serial sawtooth Fourier series code.

Appendix

The following are two exotic, rapidly converging, infinite series π equations from the famed Ramanujan and the Chudnovsky brothers. These turbocharged π equations require, at most, two iterations to give a π value of fifteen decimal place accuracy. The Chudnovsky brothers' equation was derived from Ramanujan's formula, and the Chudnovsky algorithm was used in December 2009 to calculate π to an accuracy of 2.7 trillion digit, five trillion digits in August 2010, ten trillion digits in October 2011, and 12.1 trillion digits in December 2013. For a more in-depth historical perspective, please see the following links:

- https://en.wikipedia.org/wiki/Chudnovsky_algorithm
- https://en.m.wikipedia.org/wiki/Chudnovsky_brothers
- https://en.m.wikipedia.org/wiki/Approximations_of_%CF%80
- https://en.wikipedia.org/wiki/Srinivasa_Ramanujan
- https://en.wikipedia.org/wiki/Pi
- https://en.wikipedia.org/wiki/List_of_formulae_involving_%CF%80
- https://crypto.stanford.edu/pbc/notes/pi/ramanujan.html
- https://www.youtube.com/watch?v=ZoaEPXEcLFI

The Ramanujan infinite series formula is as follows:

$$\frac{1}{\pi} = \frac{2\sqrt{2}}{9801} \sum_{k=0}^{\infty} \frac{(4k)!\,(1103 + 26390k)}{k!^4\, 396^{4k}}$$

Its MPI code and how it runs are depicted on the following pages:

```
/*********************************************
 * Ramanujan MPI pi code. *
 * *
 * This infinite seriesconverges rapidly. *
 * Only two iterations for *
 * 15 decimalplace accuracy. *
 * *
 * Author: Carlos R. Morrison *
 * *
 * Date: 1/11/2017 *
 *********************************************/
```

```c
#include<mpi.h>// (Open)MPI library
#include<math.h>// math library
#include<stdio.h>// Standard Input/Output library

int main(int argc, char*argv[])
{
 int total_iter;
 int n,rank,length,numprocs;
 double pi,sum,sum0,x,rank_sum,A,B,C,D,E;
 char hostname[MPI_MAX_PROCESSOR_NAME];

 unsignedlong factorial(unsignedlong number);
 unsignedlonglong i,j,k,l,m;
 double F = 2.0*sqrt(2.0)/9801.0;

 MPI_Init(&argc, &argv); // initiates MPI
 MPI_Comm_size(MPI_COMM_WORLD, &numprocs); // acquire number of
 processes
 MPI_Comm_rank(MPI_COMM_WORLD, &rank); // acquire current process id
 MPI_Get_processor_name(hostname, &length); // acquire hostname

if (rank == 0)
 {
  printf("\n");
  printf("##########################################################");
  printf("\n\n\n");
  printf("*** NUMBER OF PROCESSORS: %d\n",numprocs);
  printf("\n\n");
  printf("MASTER NODE NAME: %s\n", hostname);
  printf("\n");
  printf("Enter the number of iterations:\n");
  printf("\n");
  scanf("%d",&n);
  printf("\n");
 }

// broadcast to all processes, the number of segments you want
 MPI_Bcast(&n, 1, MPI_INT, 0, MPI_COMM_WORLD);

// this loop increments the maximum number of iterations, thus providing
// additional work for testing computational speed of the processors
// for(total_iter = 1; total_iter < n; total_iter++)
 {
 sum0 = 0.0;
// for(i = rank + 1; i <= total_iter; i += numprocs)
for(i = rank + 1; i <= n; i += numprocs)
 {
  k = i-1;
```

```
    A = 1;
for(l=1; l <= 4*k; l++)// (4*k)!
 {
  A *= l;
 }

 B = (double)(1103+26390*k);

 C = 1;
for(m=1; m <= k; m++)// k!
 {
  C *= m;
 }

 D = (double)pow(396,4*k);
 E = (double)A*B/(C*D);

 sum0 += E;

 }// End of for(i = rank + 1; i <= total_iter; i += numprocs)

 rank_sum = sum0;// Partial sum for a given rank

// collect and add the partial sum0 values from all processes
 MPI_Reduce(&rank_sum, &sum, 1, MPI_DOUBLE,MPI_SUM, 0, MPI_COMM_WORLD);

 } // End of for(total_iter = 1; total_iter < n; total_iter++)

if(rank == 0)
 {
  pi = 1.0/(F*sum);
  printf("\n\n");
  /* printf("*** Number of processes: %d\n",numprocs);
  printf("\n\n");*/
  printf(" Calculated pi = %.16f\n", pi);
  printf(" M_PI = %.16f\n", M_PI);
  printf(" Relative Error = %.16f\n", fabs(pi-M_PI));
 }

  // clean up, done with MPI
  MPI_Finalize();

 return 0;
}// End of int main(int argc, char*argv[])

alpha@Mst0:/beta/gamma $ time mpiexec -H
Mst0,Slv1,Slv2,Slv3,Slv4,Slv5,Slv6,Slv7,Slv8,
Slv9,Slv10,Slv11,Slv12,Slv13,Slv14,Slv15 Ramanujan
```

```
##########################################################


*** NUMBER OF PROCESSORS: 16


MASTER NODE NAME: Mst0

Enter the number of iterations:

2



Calculated pi = 3.1415926535897936
 M_PI = 3.1415926535897931
 Relative Error = 0.0000000000000004

real 0m8.974s
user 0m1.200s
sys 0m0.360s
```

The Chudnovsky infinite series formula is as follows:

$$\frac{1}{\pi} = \frac{12}{640320^{3/2}} \sum_{k=0}^{\infty} \frac{(6k)!\,(13591409 + 545140134k)}{(3k)!\,(k!)^3(-640320)^{3k}}$$

Its MPI code and how it runs are depicted on the following pages:

```
/*********************************************
 * Chudnovsky MPI pi code. *
 *
 * This infinite series converges rapidly.*
 * Only two iterations for 15 decimal *
 * place accuracy. *
 *
 * Author: Carlos R. Morrison *
 *
 * Date: 1/11/2017 *
 *********************************************/

#include<mpi.h>// (Open)MPI library

#include<math.h>// math library

#include<stdio.h>// Standard Input/Output library
```

```c
int main(int argc, char*argv[])

{

   int total_iter;

   int n,rank,length,numprocs;

   double pi;

   double sum0,x,rank_sum,A,B,C,D,E,G,H;

   double F = 12.0/pow(640320,1.5),sum;

   unsignedlonglong i,j,k,l,m;

   char hostname[MPI_MAX_PROCESSOR_NAME];

   MPI_Init(&argc, &argv); // initiates MPI

   MPI_Comm_size(MPI_COMM_WORLD, &numprocs); // acquire number of
   processes

   MPI_Comm_rank(MPI_COMM_WORLD, &rank); // acquire current process id

   MPI_Get_processor_name(hostname, &length); // acquire hostname

if (rank == 0)

 {
  printf("\n");
  printf("#####################################################");
  printf("\n\n\n");
  printf("*** NUMBER OF PROCESSORS: %d\n",numprocs);
  printf("\n\n");
  printf("MASTER NODE NAME: %s\n", hostname);
  printf("\n");
  printf("Enter the number of iterations:\n");
  printf("\n");
  scanf("%d",&n);
  printf("\n");
 }

 // broadcast to all processes, the number of segments you want

  MPI_Bcast(&n, 1, MPI_INT, 0, MPI_COMM_WORLD);
 // this loop increments the maximum number of iterations, thus
  providing
```

```
// additional work for testing computational speed of the processors

// for(total_iter = 1; total_iter < n; total_iter++)

{
  sum0 = 0.0;
  // for(i = rank + 1; i <= total_iter; i += numprocs)
   for(i = rank + 1; i <= n; i += numprocs)
   {
      k = i-1;
      A = 1;

   for(j=1; j <= 6*k; j++)// (6*k)!
   {
      A *= j;
   }
      B = (double)(13591409+545140134*k);
      C = 1;

   for(l=1; l <= 3*k; l++)// (3k)!
   {
      C *= l;
   }

      D = 1;

   for(m=1; m <= k; m++)// k!
   {
      D *= m;
   }

   E = pow(D,3);// (k!)^3
   G = (double)pow(-640320,3*k);
   H = (double)A*B/(C*E*G);

   sum0 += H;
  }// End of for(i = rank + 1; i <= total_iter; i += numprocs)

   rank_sum = sum0;// Partial sum for a given rank

   // collect and add the partial sum0 values from all processes

   MPI_Reduce(&rank_sum, &sum, 1, MPI_DOUBLE,MPI_SUM, 0,
   MPI_COMM_WORLD);

  } // End of for(total_iter = 1; total_iter < n; total_iter++)

 if(rank == 0)
```

```
{
  printf("\n\n");
  // printf("*** Number of processes: %d\n",numprocs);
  // printf("\n\n");
  pi = 1.0/(F*sum);
  printf(" Calculated pi = %.16f\n", pi);
  printf(" M_PI = %.16f\n", M_PI);
  printf(" Relative Error = %.16f\n", fabs(pi-M_PI));
}

// clean up, done with MPI

MPI_Finalize();

return 0;

}// End of int main(int argc, char*argv[])
```

alpha@Mst0:/beta/gamma $ time mpiexec -H
Mst0,Slv1,Slv2,Slv3,Slv4,Slv5,Slv6,Slv7,Slv8,

Slv9,Slv10,Slv11,Slv12,Slv13,Slv14,Slv15 Chudnovsky

###

*** NUMBER OF PROCESSORS: 16

MASTER NODE NAME: Mst0

Enter the number of iterations:

2

Calculated pi = 3.1415926535897936

M_PI = 3.1415926535897931

Relative Error = 0.0000000000000004

real 0m5.155s

user 0m1.220s

sys 0m0.340s

alpha@Mst0:/beta/gamma $

Go ahead, copy/write and the run the following codes; one of them is very efficient for the number of iteration required to generate a very accurate value for π:

Unknown:

$$\pi = \sum_{k=0}^{\infty} \frac{8}{(4k+1)(4k+3)},$$

Simon Pluff:

$$\pi = \sum_{k=0}^{\infty} \frac{1}{16^k}\left(\frac{4}{8k+1} - \frac{2}{8k+4} - \frac{1}{8k+5} - \frac{1}{8k+6}\right)$$

Fabrice — Bellard:

$$\pi = \frac{1}{2^6} \sum_{k=0}^{\infty} \frac{(-1)^k}{2^{10k}}\left(-\frac{2^5}{4k+1} - \frac{1}{4k+3} + \frac{2^8}{10k+1} - \frac{2^6}{10k+3} - \frac{2^2}{10k+5} - \frac{2^2}{10k+7} + \frac{1}{10k+9}\right)$$

Definitions

- **Core** – A core is a processing unit that reads in instructions to perform specific actions
- **Cluster** – A cluster is a set of connected computers that work together as a single unit
- **New Out Of Box Software (NOOBS)** – Term usually associated with the Raspberry Pi microcomputer software
- **Node** – A node is a single computer
- **Raspbian** – This is the Raspberry Pi foundation's official supported OS
- **Super cluster** – Used interchangeably with supercomputer
- **Thread** – A thread is a single line of command that is being processed

Index

U

V

85120264R00141